MW01180965

THE GOSPEL MESSAGE

Chronological & Abridged

Compiled by

John Mark Morgan, Ph.D.

Todd—
Thanks for your
support and encouragement
Mark

xulon
PRESS

Copyright © 2012 by John Mark Morgan, Ph.D.

The Gospel Message
Chronological and Abridged
by John Mark Morgan, Ph.D.

Printed in the United States of America

ISBN 9781619964686

All rights reserved solely by the author. The author guarantees all contents are original and do not infringe upon the legal rights of any other person or work. No part of this book may be reproduced in any form without the permission of the author. The views expressed in this book are not necessarily those of the publisher.

Unless otherwise indicated, Bible quotations are taken from The *World English Bible*™. http://ebible.org/.

www.xulonpress.com

Acknowledgements

◎ ◎ ◎

Writing a book is like planting a garden - it takes a long time for the seed to bear fruit, ready for harvest and off to the market. Every detail is important, including color, size, texture, and taste. Although one person can be a successful gardener, the task becomes easy and the joy widespread when others help. I am grateful for the contributions of many people who tended my "garden."

My immediate family has been a source of encouragement ever since this idea germinated. Sincere thanks to my wife Karen, and Meredith & Jonathan (kids) for your love and support. My mother (Joyce) and sisters (Mary & Jane) provided me with some good ideas and advice during cultivation. Closer to harvest, several pastors and full-time Christian servants assured me that the fruit was ripe and ready for picking. Those individuals include, Kevin Glenn, Bob Arthur, Drew Martin, David Allen, Paul Larimore, Todd Pridemore, Bob Lively, and Walter Tillman.

In closing, I would like to dedicate this book to my late father, Bobby E. Morgan (1931–2011). Dad would have enjoyed seeing this book in print because his life story was about Christianity.

Table of Contents

◉ ◉ ◉

Introduction

◎ ◎ ◎

Although Jesus Christ changed the course of human history, some people have not heard about God's only Son whose message of hope is found in the first four books of the New Testament. This collection of scriptures, also known as the Gospels, literally means the Good News. It reveals God's plan of salvation through the life, ministry, and teachings of Jesus Christ. *"For God so loved the world, that he gave his one and only Son, that whoever believes in him should not perish, but have eternal life"* (John 3: 16).

God chose ordinary people and empowered them to write the Gospels. Each of these books were written several decades after the death and resurrection of Jesus Christ by authors using oral testimony, eyewitness accounts, and other sources of reliable information. Many stories were recorded more than once, but others consist of a single entry. The Gospel writers provide insight on Jesus Christ and His disciples not found elsewhere in the *Holy Bible*. Readers should expect to find some variation in the sequence and detail of events presented by the authors, perhaps due to differences in their occupations, personalities, and writing styles. However, "Every Scripture is God-breathed and profitable for teaching, for reproof, for correction, and for instruction in righteousness" (2 Timothy 3: 16).

Luke addressed some of these issues in the preface of his book. "Since many have undertaken to set in order a narrative concerning those matters which have been fulfilled among us, even as those who from the beginning were eyewitnesses and servants of the word delivered them to us, it seemed good to me also, having traced the course of all things accurately from the first, to write to you in order, most excellent Theophilus; that you might know the certainty concerning the things in which you were instructed" (Luke 1: 1-4).

The Gospel Message is a seamless narrative, designed to reflect a four-fold purpose: 1) to provide a chronology of Matthew, Mark, Luke, and John; 2) to tell the story of Jesus Christ; 3) to condense the information by removing duplications; and 4) to improve readability by using a modern-day translation of the *Holy Bible*. God's word, when presented in this manner, makes it easy for people to learn about Jesus and His redemptive purpose. Its relevance spans across time and culture. For, "All flesh is like grass, and all of man's glory like the flower in the grass. The grass withers, and its flower falls; but the Lord's word endures forever." This is the word of Good News which was preached to you (1 Peter 1: 24-25).

Near the end of Jesus' public ministry He prayed, *"Righteous Father, the world hasn't known you, but I knew you; and these knew that you sent me. I made known to them your name, and will make it known; that the love with which you loved me may be in them, and I in them"* (John 17: 25-26). I have selected this passage as the vision statement for *The Gospel Message*.

I encourage you to read this book and share it with others. All scripture passages were taken from the *World English Bible*™ (WEB), a modern-day translation of the *American Standard Version*. The WEB is in the public domain and can be found on-line at http://ebible.org/

The Word Becomes Flesh
- **John 1: 1-5**

[1] In the beginning was the Word, and the Word was with God, and the Word was God. [2] The same was in the beginning with God. [3] All things were made through him. Without him was not anything made that has been made. [4] In him was life, and the life was the light of men. [5] The light shines in the darkness, and the darkness hasn't overcome it.

The Birth of John the Baptist Foretold
- **Luke 1: 5-25**

[5] There was in the days of Herod, the king of Judea, a certain priest named Zacharias, of the priestly division of Abijah. He had a wife of the daughters of Aaron, and her name was Elizabeth. [6] They were both righteous before God, walking blamelessly in all the commandments and ordinances of the Lord. [7] But they had no child, because Elizabeth was barren, and they both were well advanced in years. [8] Now it happened, while he executed the priest's office before God in the order of his division, [9] according to the custom of the priest's office, his lot was to enter into the temple of the Lord and burn incense. [10] The whole multitude of the people were praying outside at the hour of incense. [11] An angel of the Lord appeared to him, standing on the right side of the altar of incense. [12] Zacharias was troubled when he saw him, and fear fell upon him. [13] But the angel said to him, "Don't be afraid, Zacharias, because your request has been heard, and your wife, Elizabeth, will bear you a son, and you shall call his name John. [14] You will have joy and gladness; and

many will rejoice at his birth. [15] For he will be great in the sight of the Lord, and he will drink no wine nor strong drink. He will be filled with the Holy Spirit, even from his mother's womb. [16] He will turn many of the children of Israel to the Lord, their God. [17] He will go before him in the spirit and power of Elijah, 'to turn the hearts of the fathers to the children,' and the disobedient to the wisdom of the just; to prepare a people prepared for the Lord." [18] Zacharias said to the angel, "How can I be sure of this? For I am an old man, and my wife is well advanced in years." [19] The angel answered him, "I am Gabriel, who stands in the presence of God. I was sent to speak to you, and to bring you this good news. [20] Behold, you will be silent and not able to speak, until the day that these things will happen, because you didn't believe my words, which will be fulfilled in their proper time." [21] The people were waiting for Zacharias, and they marveled that he delayed in the temple. [22] When he came out, he could not speak to them, and they perceived that he had seen a vision in the temple. He continued making signs to them, and remained mute. [23] It happened, when the days of his service were fulfilled, he departed to his house. [24] After these days Elizabeth, his wife, conceived, and she hid herself five months, saying, [25] "Thus has the Lord done to me in the days in which he looked at me, to take away my reproach among men."

The Birth of Jesus Foretold
  • **Luke 1: 26-38**

[26] Now in the sixth month, the angel Gabriel was sent from God to a city of Galilee, named Nazareth, [27] to a virgin pledged to be married to a man whose name was Joseph, of the house of David. The virgin's name was Mary. [28] Having come in, the angel said to her, "Rejoice, you highly favored one! The Lord is with you. Blessed are you among women!" [29] But when she saw him, she was greatly troubled at the saying, and considered what kind of salutation this might be. [30] The angel said to her, "Don't be afraid, Mary, for you have found favor with God. [31] Behold, you will conceive in your womb, and bring forth a son, and will call his name 'Jesus.' [32] He will be great, and will be called the Son of the Most High. The Lord God will give him the throne of his father, David, [33] and he will reign over

the house of Jacob forever. There will be no end to his Kingdom." [34] Mary said to the angel, "How can this be, seeing I am a virgin?" [35] The angel answered her, "The Holy Spirit will come on you, and the power of the Most High will overshadow you. Therefore also the holy one who is born from you will be called the Son of God. [36] Behold, Elizabeth, your relative, also has conceived a son in her old age; and this is the sixth month with her who was called barren. [37] For everything spoken by God is possible." [38] Mary said, "Behold, the handmaid of the Lord; be it to me according to your word." The angel departed from her.

Mary and Elizabeth
- ### Luke 1: 39-56

[39] Mary arose in those days and went into the hill country with haste, into a city of Judah, [40] and entered into the house of Zacharias and greeted Elizabeth. [41] It happened, when Elizabeth heard Mary's greeting, that the baby leaped in her womb, and Elizabeth was filled with the Holy Spirit. [42] She called out with a loud voice, and said, "Blessed are you among women, and blessed is the fruit of your womb! [43] Why am I so favored, that the mother of my Lord should come to me? [44] For behold, when the voice of your greeting came into my ears, the baby leaped in my womb for joy! [45] Blessed is she who believed, for there will be a fulfillment of the things which have been spoken to her from the Lord!" [46] Mary said, "My soul magnifies the Lord. [47] My spirit has rejoiced in God my Savior, [48] for he has looked at the humble state of his handmaid. For behold, from now on, all generations will call me blessed. [49] For he who is mighty has done great things for me. Holy is his name. [50] His mercy is for generations of generations on those who fear him. [51] He has shown strength with his arm. He has scattered the proud in the imagination of their hearts. [52] He has put down princes from their thrones. And has exalted the lowly. [53] He has filled the hungry with good things. He has sent the rich away empty. [54] He has given help to Israel, his servant, that he might remember mercy, [55] As he spoke to our fathers, to Abraham and his seed forever." [56] Mary stayed with her about three months, and then returned to her house.

The Birth of John the Baptist
- ## Luke 1: 57-80

[57] Now the time that Elizabeth should give birth was fulfilled, and she brought forth a son. [58] Her neighbors and her relatives heard that the Lord had magnified his mercy towards her, and they rejoiced with her. [59] It happened on the eighth day, that they came to circumcise the child; and they would have called him Zacharias, after the name of the father. [60] His mother answered, "Not so; but he will be called John." [61] They said to her, "There is no one among your relatives who is called by this name." [62] They made signs to his father, what he would have him called. [63] He asked for a writing tablet, and wrote, "His name is John." They all marveled. [64] His mouth was opened immediately, and his tongue freed, and he spoke, blessing God. [65] Fear came on all who lived around them, and all these sayings were talked about throughout all the hill country of Judea. [66] All who heard them laid them up in their heart, saying, "What then will this child be?" The hand of the Lord was with him. [67] His father, Zacharias, was filled with the Holy Spirit, and prophesied, saying, [68] "Blessed be the Lord, the God of Israel, for he has visited and worked redemption for his people; [69] and has raised up a horn of salvation for us in the house of his servant David [70] (as he spoke by the mouth of his holy prophets who have been from of old), [71] salvation from our enemies, and from the hand of all who hate us; [72] to show mercy towards our fathers, to remember his holy covenant, [73] the oath which he spoke to Abraham, our father, [74] to grant to us that we, being delivered out of the hand of our enemies, should serve him without fear, [75] In holiness and righteousness before him all the days of our life. [76] And you, child, will be called a prophet of the Most High, for you will go before the face of the Lord to prepare his ways, [77] to give knowledge of salvation to his people by the remission of their sins, [78] because of the tender mercy of our God, whereby the dawn from on high will visit us, [79] to shine on those who sit in darkness and the shadow of death; to guide our feet into the way of peace." [80] The child was growing, and becoming strong in spirit, and was in the desert until the day of his public appearance to Israel.

An Angel Appears Before Joseph
  • **Matthew 1: 18-25**

[18] Now the birth of Jesus Christ was like this; for after his mother, Mary, was engaged to Joseph, before they came together, she was found pregnant by the Holy Spirit. [19] Joseph, her husband, being a righteous man, and not willing to make her a public example, intended to put her away secretly. [20] But when he thought about these things, behold, an angel of the Lord appeared to him in a dream, saying, "Joseph, son of David, don't be afraid to take to yourself Mary, your wife, for that which is conceived in her is of the Holy Spirit. [21] She shall bring forth a son. You shall call his name Jesus, for it is he who shall save his people from their sins." [22] Now all this has happened, that it might be fulfilled which was spoken by the Lord through the prophet, saying, [23] "Behold, the virgin shall be with child, and shall bring forth a son. They shall call his name Immanuel"; which is, being interpreted, "God with us." [24] Joseph arose from his sleep, and did as the angel of the Lord commanded him, and took his wife to himself; [25] and didn't know her sexually until she had brought forth her firstborn son. He named him Jesus.

The Birth of Jesus
  • **Luke 2: 1-7**

[1] Now it happened in those days, that a decree went out from Caesar Augustus that all the world should be enrolled. [2] This was the first enrollment made when Quirinius was governor of Syria. [3] All went to enroll themselves, everyone to his own city. [4] Joseph also went up from Galilee, out of the city of Nazareth, into Judea, to the city of David, which is called Bethlehem, because he was of the house and family of David; [5] to enroll himself with Mary, who was pledged to be married to him as wife, being pregnant. [6] It happened, while they were there, that the day had come that she should give birth. [7] She brought forth her firstborn son, and she wrapped him in bands of cloth, and laid him in a feeding trough, because there was no room for them in the inn.

Shepherds and Angels
- ## Luke 2: 8-20

[8] There were shepherds in the same country staying in the field, and keeping watch by night over their flock. [9] Behold, an angel of the Lord stood by them, and the glory of the Lord shone around them, and they were terrified. [10] The angel said to them, "Don't be afraid, for behold, I bring you good news of great joy which will be to all the people. [11] For there is born to you, this day, in the city of David, a Savior, who is Christ the Lord. [12] This is the sign to you: you will find a baby wrapped in strips of cloth, lying in a feeding trough." [13] Suddenly, there was with the angel a multitude of the heavenly army praising God, and saying, [14] "Glory to God in the highest, on earth peace, good will toward men." [15] It happened, when the angels went away from them into the sky, that the shepherds said one to another, "Let's go to Bethlehem, now, and see this thing that has happened, which the Lord has made known to us." [16] They came with haste, and found both Mary and Joseph, and the baby was lying in the feeding trough. [17] When they saw it, they publicized widely the saying which was spoken to them about this child. [18] All who heard it wondered at the things which were spoken to them by the shepherds. [19] But Mary kept all these sayings, pondering them in her heart. [20] The shepherds returned, glorifying and praising God for all the things that they had heard and seen, just as it was told them.

Baby Jesus Presented at the Temple
- ## Luke 2: 21-38

[21] When eight days were fulfilled for the circumcision of the child, his name was called Jesus, which was given by the angel before he was conceived in the womb. [22] When the days of their purification according to the law of Moses were fulfilled, they brought him up to Jerusalem, to present him to the Lord [23] (as it is written in the law of the Lord, "Every male who opens the womb shall be called holy to the Lord"), [24] and to offer a sacrifice according to that which is said in the law of the Lord, "A pair of turtledoves, or two young pigeons." [25] Behold, there was a man in Jerusalem whose name was Simeon. This man was righteous and devout, looking for the consolation of Israel, and the Holy Spirit was on him. [26] It had been revealed to him

by the Holy Spirit that he should not see death before he had seen the Lord's Christ. [27] He came in the Spirit into the temple. When the parents brought in the child, Jesus, that they might do concerning him according to the custom of the law, [28] then he received him into his arms, and blessed God, and said, [29] "Now you are releasing your servant, Master, according to your word, in peace; [30] for my eyes have seen your salvation, [31] which you have prepared before the face of all peoples; [32] a light for revelation to the nations, and the glory of your people Israel." [33] Joseph and his mother were marveling at the things which were spoken concerning him, [34] and Simeon blessed them, and said to Mary, his mother, "Behold, this child is set for the falling and the rising of many in Israel, and for a sign which is spoken against. [35] Yes, a sword will pierce through your own soul, that the thoughts of many hearts may be revealed." [36] There was one Anna, a prophetess, the daughter of Phanuel, of the tribe of Asher (she was of a great age, having lived with a husband seven years from her virginity, [37] and she had been a widow for about eighty-four years), who didn't depart from the temple, worshiping with fastings and petitions night and day. [38] Coming up at that very hour, she gave thanks to the Lord, and spoke of him to all those who were looking for redemption in Jerusalem.

Wise Men Visit the Messiah
- **Matthew 2: 1-12**

[1] Now when Jesus was born in Bethlehem of Judea in the days of King Herod, behold, wise men from the east came to Jerusalem, saying, [2] "Where is he who is born King of the Jews? For we saw his star in the east, and have come to worship him." [3] When King Herod heard it, he was troubled, and all Jerusalem with him. [4] Gathering together all the chief priests and scribes of the people, he asked them where the Christ would be born. [5] They said to him, "In Bethlehem of Judea, for this is written through the prophet, [6] 'You Bethlehem, land of Judah, are in no way least among the princes of Judah: for out of you shall come forth a governor, who shall shepherd my people, Israel.'" [7] Then Herod secretly called the wise men, and learned from them exactly what time the star appeared. [8] He sent them to Bethlehem, and said, "Go and search diligently for the young child.

When you have found him, bring me word, so that I also may come and worship him." [9] They, having heard the king, went their way; and behold, the star, which they saw in the east, went before them, until it came and stood over where the young child was. [10] When they saw the star, they rejoiced with exceedingly great joy. [11] They came into the house and saw the young child with Mary, his mother, and they fell down and worshiped him. Opening their treasures, they offered to him gifts: gold, frankincense, and myrrh. [12] Being warned in a dream that they shouldn't return to Herod, they went back to their own country another way.

Escape Into Egypt
- **Matthew 2: 13-18**

[13] Now when they had departed, behold, an angel of the Lord appeared to Joseph in a dream, saying, "Arise and take the young child and his mother, and flee into Egypt, and stay there until I tell you, for Herod will seek the young child to destroy him." [14] He arose and took the young child and his mother by night, and departed into Egypt, [15] and was there until the death of Herod; that it might be fulfilled which was spoken by the Lord through the prophet, saying, "Out of Egypt I called my son." [16] Then Herod, when he saw that he was mocked by the wise men, was exceedingly angry, and sent out, and killed all the male children who were in Bethlehem and in all the surrounding countryside, from two years old and under, according to the exact time which he had learned from the wise men. [17] Then that which was spoken by Jeremiah the prophet was fulfilled, saying, [18] "A voice was heard in Ramah, lamentation, weeping and great mourning, Rachel weeping for her children; she wouldn't be comforted, because they are no more."

Return to Nazareth
- **Matthew 2: 19-23 (Luke 2: 39-40)**

[19] But when Herod was dead, behold, an angel of the Lord appeared in a dream to Joseph in Egypt, saying, [20] "Arise and take the young child and his mother, and go into the land of Israel, for those who sought the young child's life are dead." [21] He arose and took the young child and his mother, and came into the land of Israel. [22] But

when he heard that Archelaus was reigning over Judea in the place of his father, Herod, he was afraid to go there. Being warned in a dream, he withdrew into the region of Galilee, [23] and came and lived in a city called Nazareth; that it might be fulfilled which was spoken through the prophets: "He will be called a Nazarene."

The Boy Jesus at the Temple
 • **Luke 2: 41-52**

[41] His parents went every year to Jerusalem at the feast of the Passover. [42] When he was twelve years old, they went up to Jerusalem according to the custom of the feast, [43] and when they had fulfilled the days, as they were returning, the boy Jesus stayed behind in Jerusalem. Joseph and his mother didn't know it, [44] but supposing him to be in the company, they went a day's journey, and they looked for him among their relatives and acquaintances. [45] When they didn't find him, they returned to Jerusalem, looking for him. [46] It happened after three days they found him in the temple, sitting in the midst of the teachers, both listening to them, and asking them questions. [47] All who heard him were amazed at his understanding and his answers. [48] When they saw him, they were astonished, and his mother said to him, "Son, why have you treated us this way? Behold, your father and I were anxiously looking for you." [49] He said to them, *"Why were you looking for me? Didn't you know that I must be in my Father's house?"* [50] They didn't understand the saying which he spoke to them. [51] And he went down with them, and came to Nazareth. He was subject to them, and his mother kept all these sayings in her heart. [52] And Jesus increased in wisdom and stature, and in favor with God and men.

Witness to the Light
 • **John 1: 6-18**

[6] There came a man, sent from God, whose name was John. [7] The same came as a witness, that he might testify about the light, that all might believe through him. [8] He was not the light, but was sent that he might testify about the light. [9] The true light that enlightens everyone was coming into the world. [10] He was in the world, and the world was made through him, and the world didn't recognize him.

[11] He came to his own, and those who were his own didn't receive him. [12] But as many as received him, to them he gave the right to become God's children, to those who believe in his name: [13] who were born not of blood, nor of the will of the flesh, nor of the will of man, but of God. [14] The Word became flesh, and lived among us. We saw his glory, such glory as of the one and only Son of the Father, full of grace and truth. [15] John testified about him. He cried out, saying, "This was he of whom I said, 'He who comes after me has surpassed me, for he was before me.'" [16] From his fullness we all received grace upon grace. [17] For the law was given through Moses. Grace and truth were realized through Jesus Christ. [18] No one has seen God at any time. The one and only Son, who is in the bosom of the Father, he has declared him.

John the Baptist Prepares the Way
  • **Luke 3: 1-17 (Matthew 3: 1-12; Mark 1: 1-8; John 1: 19-28)**

[1] Now in the fifteenth year of the reign of Tiberius Caesar, Pontius Pilate being governor of Judea, and Herod being tetrarch of Galilee, and his brother Philip tetrarch of the region of Ituraea and Trachonitis, and Lysanias tetrarch of Abilene, [2] in the high priesthood of Annas and Caiaphas, the word of God came to John, the son of Zacharias, in the wilderness. [3] He came into all the region around the Jordan, preaching the baptism of repentance for remission of sins. [4] As it is written in the book of the words of Isaiah the prophet, "The voice of one crying in the wilderness, 'Make ready the way of the Lord. Make his paths straight. [5] Every valley will be filled. Every mountain and hill will be brought low. The crooked will become straight, and the rough ways smooth. [6] All flesh will see God's salvation.'" [7] He said therefore to the multitudes who went out to be baptized by him, "You offspring of vipers, who warned you to flee from the wrath to come? [8] Bring forth therefore fruits worthy of repentance, and don't begin to say among yourselves, 'We have Abraham for our father;' for I tell you that God is able to raise up children to Abraham from these stones! [9] Even now the axe also lies at the root of the trees. Every tree therefore that doesn't bring forth good fruit is cut down, and thrown into the fire." [10] The multitudes asked him,

"What then must we do?" [11] He answered them, "He who has two coats, let him give to him who has none. He who has food, let him do likewise." [12] Tax collectors also came to be baptized, and they said to him, "Teacher, what must we do?" [13] He said to them, "Collect no more than that which is appointed to you." [14] Soldiers also asked him, saying, "What about us? What must we do?" He said to them, "Extort from no one by violence, neither accuse anyone wrongfully. Be content with your wages." [15] As the people were in expectation, and all men reasoned in their hearts concerning John, whether perhaps he was the Christ, [16] John answered them all, "I indeed baptize you with water, but he comes who is mightier than I, the latchet of whose sandals I am not worthy to loosen. He will baptize you in the Holy Spirit and fire, [17] whose fan is in his hand, and he will thoroughly cleanse his threshing floor, and will gather the wheat into his barn; but he will burn up the chaff with unquenchable fire."

The Baptism of Jesus
- **Matthew 3: 13-17 (Mark 1: 9-11; Luke 3: 21-22)**

[13] Then Jesus came from Galilee to the Jordan to John, to be baptized by him. [14] But John would have hindered him, saying, "I need to be baptized by you, and you come to me?" [15] But Jesus, answering, said to him, *"Allow it now, for this is the fitting way for us to fulfill all righteousness."* Then he allowed him. [16] Jesus, when he was baptized, went up directly from the water: and behold, the heavens were opened to him. He saw the Spirit of God descending as a dove, and coming on him. [17] Behold, a voice out of the heavens said, "This is my beloved Son, with whom I am well pleased."

John's Testimony
- **John 1: 29-34**

[29] The next day, he saw Jesus coming to him, and said, "Behold, the Lamb of God, who takes away the sin of the world! [30] This is he of whom I said, 'After me comes a man who is preferred before me, for he was before me.' [31] I didn't know him, but for this reason I came baptizing in water: that he would be revealed to Israel." [32] John testified, saying, "I have seen the Spirit descending like a dove out of heaven, and it remained on him. [33] I didn't recognize him, but he

who sent me to baptize in water, he said to me, 'On whomever you will see the Spirit descending, and remaining on him, the same is he who baptizes in the Holy Spirit.' [34] I have seen, and have testified that this is the Son of God."

The Genealogy of Jesus (via Mary)
  * **Luke 3: 23-38**

[23] Jesus himself, when he began to teach, was about thirty years old, being the son (as was supposed) of Joseph, the son of Heli, [24] the son of Matthat, the son of Levi, the son of Melchi, the son of Jannai, the son of Joseph, [25] the son of Mattathias, the son of Amos, the son of Nahum, the son of Esli, the son of Naggai, [26] the son of Maath, the son of Mattathias, the son of Semein, the son of Joseph, the son of Judah, [27] the son of Joanan, the son of Rhesa, the son of Zerubbabel, the son of Shealtiel, the son of Neri, [28] the son of Melchi, the son of Addi, the son of Cosam, the son of Elmodam, the son of Er, [29] the son of Jose, the son of Eliezer, the son of Jorim, the son of Matthat, the son of Levi, [30] the son of Simeon, the son of Judah, the son of Joseph, the son of Jonan, the son of Eliakim, [31] the son of Melea, the son of Menan, the son of Mattatha, the son of Nathan, the son of David, [32] the son of Jesse, the son of Obed, the son of Boaz, the son of Salmon, the son of Nahshon, [33] the son of Amminadab, the son of Aram, the son of Hezron, the son of Perez, the son of Judah, [34] the son of Jacob, the son of Isaac, the son of Abraham, the son of Terah, the son of Nahor, [35] the son of Serug, the son of Reu, the son of Peleg, the son of Eber, the son of Shelah, [36] the son of Cainan, the son of Arphaxad, the son of Shem, the son of Noah, the son of Lamech, [37] the son of Methuselah, the son of Enoch, the son of Jared, the son of Mahalaleel, the son of Cainan, [38] the son of Enos, the son of Seth, the son of Adam, the son of God.

The Genealogy of Jesus (via Joseph)
  * **Matthew 1: 1-17**

[1] The book of the genealogy of Jesus Christ, the son of David, the son of Abraham. [2] Abraham became the father of Isaac. Isaac became the father of Jacob. Jacob became the father of Judah and his brothers. [3] Judah became the father of Perez and Zerah by Tamar. Perez became

the father of Hezron. Hezron became the father of Ram. [4] Ram became the father of Amminadab. Amminadab became the father of Nahshon. Nahshon became the father of Salmon. [5] Salmon became the father of Boaz by Rahab. Boaz became the father of Obed by Ruth. Obed became the father of Jesse. [6] Jesse became the father of King David. David became the father of Solomon by her who had been the wife of Uriah. [7] Solomon became the father of Rehoboam. Rehoboam became the father of Abijah. Abijah became the father of Asa. [8] Asa became the father of Jehoshaphat. Jehoshaphat became the father of Joram. Joram became the father of Uzziah. [9] Uzziah became the father of Jotham. Jotham became the father of Ahaz. Ahaz became the father of Hezekiah. [10] Hezekiah became the father of Manasseh. Manasseh became the father of Amon. Amon became the father of Josiah. [11] Josiah became the father of Jechoniah and his brothers, at the time of the exile to Babylon. [12] After the exile to Babylon, Jechoniah became the father of Shealtiel. Shealtiel became the father of Zerubbabel. [13] Zerubbabel became the father of Abiud. Abiud became the father of Eliakim. Eliakim became the father of Azor. [14] Azor became the father of Sadoc. Sadoc became the father of Achim. Achim became the father of Eliud. [15] Eliud became the father of Eleazar. Eleazar became the father of Matthan. Matthan became the father of Jacob. [16] Jacob became the father of Joseph, the husband of Mary, from whom was born Jesus, who is called Christ. [17] So all the generations from Abraham to David are fourteen generations; from David to the exile to Babylon fourteen generations; and from the carrying away to Babylon to the Christ, fourteen generations.

Temptation in the Wilderness
  • **Luke 4: 1-13 (Matthew 4: 1-11; Mark 1: 12-13)**
[1] Jesus, full of the Holy Spirit, returned from the Jordan, and was led by the Spirit into the wilderness [2] for forty days, being tempted by the devil. He ate nothing in those days. Afterward, when they were completed, he was hungry. [3] The devil said to him, "If you are the Son of God, command this stone to become bread." [4] Jesus answered him, saying, *"It is written, 'Man shall not live by bread alone, but by every word of God.'"* [5] The devil, leading him up on a high moun-

tain, showed him all the kingdoms of the world in a moment of time.
⁶ The devil said to him, "I will give you all this authority, and their
glory, for it has been delivered to me; and I give it to whomever I
want. ⁷ If you therefore will worship before me, it will all be yours."
⁸ Jesus answered him, *"Get behind me Satan! For it is written, 'You
shall worship the Lord your God, and you shall serve him only.'"* ⁹
He led him to Jerusalem, and set him on the pinnacle of the temple,
and said to him, "If you are the Son of God, cast yourself down from
here, ¹⁰ for it is written, 'He will put his angels in charge of you, to
guard you;' ¹¹ and, 'On their hands they will bear you up, lest perhaps you dash your foot against a stone.'" ¹² Jesus answering, said to
him, *"It has been said, 'You shall not tempt the Lord your God.'"* ¹³
When the devil had completed every temptation, he departed from
him until another time.

Jesus' First Disciples
   • **John 1: 35-51**

³⁵ Again, the next day, John was standing with two of his disciples,
³⁶ and he looked at Jesus as he walked, and said, "Behold, the Lamb
of God!" ³⁷ The two disciples heard him speak, and they followed
Jesus. ³⁸ Jesus turned, and saw them following, and said to them,
"What are you looking for?" They said to him, "Rabbi" (which is
to say, being interpreted, Teacher), "where are you staying?" ³⁹ He
said to them, *"Come, and see."* They came and saw where he was
staying, and they stayed with him that day. It was about the tenth
hour. ⁴⁰ One of the two who heard John, and followed him, was
Andrew, Simon Peter's brother. ⁴¹ He first found his own brother,
Simon, and said to him, "We have found the Messiah!" (which is,
being interpreted, Christ). ⁴² He brought him to Jesus. Jesus looked
at him, and said, *"You are Simon the son of Jonah. You shall be
called Cephas"* (which is by interpretation, Peter). ⁴³ On the next
day, he was determined to go out into Galilee, and he found Philip.
Jesus said to him, *"Follow me."* ⁴⁴ Now Philip was from Bethsaida,
of the city of Andrew and Peter. ⁴⁵ Philip found Nathanael, and said
to him, "We have found him, of whom Moses in the law, and the
prophets, wrote: Jesus of Nazareth, the son of Joseph." ⁴⁶ Nathanael
said to him, "Can any good thing come out of Nazareth?" Philip said

to him, "Come and see." [47] Jesus saw Nathanael coming to him, and said about him, *"Behold, an Israelite indeed, in whom is no deceit!"* [48] Nathanael said to him, "How do you know me?" Jesus answered him, *"Before Philip called you, when you were under the fig tree, I saw you."* [49] Nathanael answered him, "Rabbi, you are the Son of God! You are King of Israel!" [50] Jesus answered him, *"Because I told you, 'I saw you underneath the fig tree,' do you believe? You will see greater things than these!"* [51] He said to him, *"Most certainly, I tell you, hereafter you will see heaven opened, and the angels of God ascending and descending on the Son of Man."*

Water Into Wine
- **John 2: 1-12**

[1] The third day, there was a marriage in Cana of Galilee. Jesus' mother was there. [2] Jesus also was invited, with his disciples, to the marriage. [3] When the wine ran out, Jesus' mother said to him, "They have no wine." [4] Jesus said to her, *"Woman, what does that have to do with you and me? My hour has not yet come."* [5] His mother said to the servants, "Whatever he says to you, do it." [6] Now there were six water pots of stone set there after the Jews' way of purifying, containing two or three metretes apiece. [7] Jesus said to them, *"Fill the water pots with water."* They filled them up to the brim. [8] He said to them, *"Now draw some out, and take it to the ruler of the feast."* So they took it. [9] When the ruler of the feast tasted the water now become wine, and didn't know where it came from (but the servants who had drawn the water knew), the ruler of the feast called the bridegroom, [10] and said to him, "Everyone serves the good wine first, and when the guests have drunk freely, then that which is worse. You have kept the good wine until now!" [11] This beginning of his signs Jesus did in Cana of Galilee, and revealed his glory; and his disciples believed in him. [12] After this, he went down to Capernaum, he, and his mother, his brothers, and his disciples; and they stayed there a few days.

Jesus Clears the Temple Courts
* **John 2: 13-25**

¹³ The Passover of the Jews was at hand, and Jesus went up to Jerusalem. ¹⁴ He found in the temple those who sold oxen, sheep, and doves, and the changers of money sitting. ¹⁵ He made a whip of cords, and threw all out of the temple, both the sheep and the oxen; and he poured out the changers' money, and overthrew their tables. ¹⁶ To those who sold the doves, he said, *"Take these things out of here! Don't make my Father's house a marketplace!"* ¹⁷ His disciples remembered that it was written, "Zeal for your house will eat me up." ¹⁸ The Jews therefore answered him, "What sign do you show us, seeing that you do these things?" ¹⁹ Jesus answered them, *"Destroy this temple, and in three days I will raise it up."* ²⁰ The Jews therefore said, "It took forty-six years to build this temple! Will you raise it up in three days?" ²¹ But he spoke of the temple of his body. ²² When therefore he was raised from the dead, his disciples remembered that he said this, and they believed the Scripture, and the word which Jesus had said. ²³ Now when he was in Jerusalem at the Passover, during the feast, many believed in his name, observing his signs which he did. ²⁴ But Jesus didn't trust himself to them, because he knew everyone, ²⁵ and because he didn't need for anyone to testify concerning man; for he himself knew what was in man.

Jesus and Nicodemus
* **John 3: 1-21**

¹ Now there was a man of the Pharisees named Nicodemus, a ruler of the Jews. ² The same came to him by night, and said to him, "Rabbi, we know that you are a teacher come from God, for no one can do these signs that you do, unless God is with him." ³ Jesus answered him, *"Most certainly, I tell you, unless one is born anew, he can't see the Kingdom of God."* ⁴ Nicodemus said to him, "How can a man be born when he is old? Can he enter a second time into his mother's womb, and be born?" ⁵ Jesus answered, *"Most certainly I tell you, unless one is born of water and spirit, he can't enter into the Kingdom of God! ⁶ That which is born of the flesh is flesh. That which is born of the Spirit is spirit. ⁷ Don't marvel that I said to you, 'You must be born anew.' ⁸ The wind blows where it wants to, and*

you hear its sound, but don't know where it comes from and where it is going. So is everyone who is born of the Spirit." [9] Nicodemus answered him, "How can these things be?" [10] Jesus answered him, *"Are you the teacher of Israel, and don't understand these things?* [11] *Most certainly I tell you, we speak that which we know, and testify of that which we have seen, and you don't receive our witness.* [12] *If I told you earthly things and you don't believe, how will you believe if I tell you heavenly things?* [13] *No one has ascended into heaven, but he who descended out of heaven, the Son of Man, who is in heaven.* [14] *As Moses lifted up the serpent in the wilderness, even so must the Son of Man be lifted up,* [15] *that whoever believes in him should not perish, but have eternal life.* [16] *For God so loved the world, that he gave his one and only Son, that whoever believes in him should not perish, but have eternal life.* [17] *For God didn't send his Son into the world to judge the world, but that the world should be saved through him.* [18] *He who believes in him is not judged. He who doesn't believe has been judged already, because he has not believed in the name of the one and only Son of God.* [19] *This is the judgment, that the light has come into the world, and men loved the darkness rather than the light; for their works were evil.* [20] *For everyone who does evil hates the light, and doesn't come to the light, lest his works would be exposed.* [21] *But he who does the truth comes to the light, that his works may be revealed, that they have been done in God."*

John the Baptist Testifies About Jesus
  • **John 3: 22-36**

[22] After these things, Jesus came with his disciples into the land of Judea. He stayed there with them, and baptized. [23] John also was baptizing in Enon near Salim, because there was much water there. They came, and were baptized. [24] For John was not yet thrown into prison. [25] There arose therefore a questioning on the part of John's disciples with some Jews about purification. [26] They came to John, and said to him, "Rabbi, he who was with you beyond the Jordan, to whom you have testified, behold, the same baptizes, and everyone is coming to him." [27] John answered, "A man can receive nothing, unless it has been given him from heaven. [28] You yourselves testify that I said, 'I am not the Christ,' but, 'I have been sent before

him.' [29] He who has the bride is the bridegroom; but the friend of the bridegroom, who stands and hears him, rejoices greatly because of the bridegroom's voice. This, my joy, therefore is made full. [30] He must increase, but I must decrease. [31] He who comes from above is above all. He who is from the earth belongs to the earth, and speaks of the earth. He who comes from heaven is above all. [32] What he has seen and heard, of that he testifies; and no one receives his witness. [33] He who has received his witness has set his seal to this, that God is true. [34] For he whom God has sent speaks the words of God; for God gives the Spirit without measure. [35] The Father loves the Son, and has given all things into his hand. [36] One who believes in the Son has eternal life, but one who disobeys the Son won't see life, but the wrath of God remains on him."

John the Baptist in Prison
  • **Luke 3: 18-20**

[18] Then with many other exhortations he preached good news to the people, [19] but Herod the tetrarch, being reproved by him for Herodias, his brother's wife, and for all the evil things which Herod had done, [20] added this also to them all, that he shut up John in prison.

A Samaritan Woman at the Well
  • **John 4: 1-42**

[1] Therefore when the Lord knew that the Pharisees had heard that Jesus was making and baptizing more disciples than John [2] (although Jesus himself didn't baptize, but his disciples), [3] he left Judea, and departed into Galilee. [4] He needed to pass through Samaria. [5] So he came to a city of Samaria, called Sychar, near the parcel of ground that Jacob gave to his son, Joseph. [6] Jacob's well was there. Jesus therefore, being tired from his journey, sat down by the well. It was about the sixth hour. [7] A woman of Samaria came to draw water. Jesus said to her, *"Give me a drink."* [8] For his disciples had gone away into the city to buy food. [9] The Samaritan woman therefore said to him, "How is it that you, being a Jew, ask for a drink from me, a Samaritan woman?" (For Jews have no dealings with Samaritans.) [10] Jesus answered her, *"If you knew the gift of God, and who it is who says to you, 'Give me a drink,' you would have asked him, and*

he would have given you living water." [11] The woman said to him, "Sir, you have nothing to draw with, and the well is deep. From where then have you that living water? [12] Are you greater than our father, Jacob, who gave us the well, and drank of it himself, as did his children, and his livestock?" [13] Jesus answered her, *"Everyone who drinks of this water will thirst again,* [14] *but whoever drinks of the water that I will give him will never thirst again; but the water that I will give him will become in him a well of water springing up to eternal life."* [15] The woman said to him, "Sir, give me this water, so that I don't get thirsty, neither come all the way here to draw." [16] Jesus said to her, *"Go, call your husband, and come here."* [17] The woman answered, "I have no husband." Jesus said to her, *"You said well, 'I have no husband,'* [18] *for you have had five husbands; and he whom you now have is not your husband. This you have said truly."* [19] The woman said to him, "Sir, I perceive that you are a prophet. [20] Our fathers worshiped in this mountain, and you Jews say that in Jerusalem is the place where people ought to worship." [21] Jesus said to her, *"Woman, believe me, the hour comes, when neither in this mountain, nor in Jerusalem, will you worship the Father. [22] You worship that which you don't know. We worship that which we know; for salvation is from the Jews. [23] But the hour comes, and now is, when the true worshipers will worship the Father in spirit and truth, for the Father seeks such to be his worshipers. [24] God is spirit, and those who worship him must worship in spirit and truth."* [25] The woman said to him, "I know that Messiah comes," (he who is called Christ). "When he has come, he will declare to us all things." [26] Jesus said to her, *"I am he, the one who speaks to you."* [27] At this, his disciples came. They marveled that he was speaking with a woman; yet no one said, "What are you looking for?" or, "Why do you speak with her?" [28] So the woman left her water pot, and went away into the city, and said to the people, [29] "Come, see a man who told me everything that I did. Can this be the Christ?" [30] They went out of the city, and were coming to him. [31] In the meanwhile, the disciples urged him, saying, "Rabbi, eat." [32] But he said to them, *"I have food to eat that you don't know about."* [33] The disciples therefore said one to another, "Has anyone brought him something to eat?" [34] Jesus said to them, *"My food is to do the will of him who sent me, and to accomplish his work. [35] Don't you say, 'There are yet four months until the harvest?' Behold, I tell you, lift up your eyes, and look at the fields, that they are white for harvest already. [36] He who reaps receives wages, and gathers fruit to eternal life; that both he who sows and he who reaps may rejoice together. [37] For in this the saying is true, 'One sows, and another reaps.' [38] I sent you to reap that for which you haven't labored. Others have labored, and you have entered into their labor."* [39] From that city many of the Samaritans believed in him because of the word of the woman, who testified, "He told me everything that I did." [40] So when the Samaritans came to him, they begged him to stay with them. He stayed there two days. [41] Many more believed because of his word. [42] They said to the woman, "Now we believe, not because of your speaking; for we have heard for ourselves, and know that this is indeed the Christ, the Savior of the world."

Jesus Begins Preaching
- **Matthew 4: 12-17 (Mark 1: 14-15; Luke 4: 14-15; John 4: 43-45)**

[12] Now when Jesus heard that John was delivered up, he withdrew into Galilee. [13] Leaving Nazareth, he came and lived in Capernaum, which is by the sea, in the region of Zebulun and Naphtali, [14] that it might be fulfilled which was spoken through Isaiah the prophet, saying, [15] "The land of Zebulun and the land of Naphtali, toward the sea, beyond the Jordan, Galilee of the Gentiles, [16] the people who sat in darkness saw a great light, to those who sat in the region and shadow of death, to them light has dawned." [17] From that time, Jesus began to preach, and to say, *"Repent! For the Kingdom of Heaven is at hand."*

A Prophet Without Honor
- **Luke 4: 16-30 (Matthew 13: 54-58; Mark 6: 1-6a)**

[16] He came to Nazareth, where he had been brought up. He entered, as was his custom, into the synagogue on the Sabbath day, and stood up to read. [17] The book of the prophet Isaiah was handed to him. He opened the book, and found the place where it was written, [18] *"The Spirit of the Lord is on me, because he has anointed me to preach*

good news to the poor. He has sent me to heal the brokenhearted, to proclaim release to the captives, recovering of sight to the blind, to deliver those who are crushed, [19] *and to proclaim the acceptable year of the Lord."* [20] He closed the book, gave it back to the attendant, and sat down. The eyes of all in the synagogue were fastened on him. [21] He began to tell them, *"Today, this Scripture has been fulfilled in your hearing."* [22] All testified about him, and wondered at the gracious words which proceeded out of his mouth, and they said, "Isn't this Joseph's son?" [23] He said to them, *"Doubtless you will tell me this parable, 'Physician, heal yourself! Whatever we have heard done at Capernaum, do also here in your hometown.'"* [24] He said, *"Most certainly I tell you, no prophet is acceptable in his hometown.* [25] *But truly I tell you, there were many widows in Israel in the days of Elijah, when the sky was shut up three years and six months, when a great famine came over all the land.* [26] *Elijah was sent to none of them, except to Zarephath, in the land of Sidon, to a woman who was a widow.* [27] *There were many lepers in Israel in the time of Elisha the prophet, yet not one of them was cleansed, except Naaman, the Syrian."* [28] They were all filled with wrath in the synagogue, as they heard these things. [29] They rose up, threw him out of the city, and led him to the brow of the hill that their city was built on, that they might throw him off the cliff. [30] But he, passing through their midst, went his way.

A Government Official's Son
   • **John 4: 46-54**

[46] Jesus came therefore again to Cana of Galilee, where he made the water into wine. There was a certain nobleman whose son was sick at Capernaum. [47] When he heard that Jesus had come out of Judea into Galilee, he went to him, and begged him that he would come down and heal his son, for he was at the point of death. [48] Jesus therefore said to him, *"Unless you see signs and wonders, you will in no way believe."* [49] The nobleman said to him, "Sir, come down before my child dies." [50] Jesus said to him, *"Go your way. Your son lives."* The man believed the word that Jesus spoke to him, and he went his way. [51] As he was now going down, his servants met him and reported, saying "Your child lives!" [52] So he inquired of them the hour when

he began to get better. They said therefore to him, "Yesterday at the seventh hour, the fever left him." [53] So the father knew that it was at that hour in which Jesus said to him, *"Your son lives."* He believed, as did his whole house. [54] This is again the second sign that Jesus did, having come out of Judea into Galilee.

Jesus Drives out an Evil Spirit
• **Mark 1: 21-28 (Luke 4: 31-37)**

[21] They went into Capernaum, and immediately on the Sabbath day he entered into the synagogue and taught. [22] They were astonished at his teaching, for he taught them as having authority, and not as the scribes. [23] Immediately there was in their synagogue a man with an unclean spirit, and he cried out, [24] saying, "Ha! What do we have to do with you, Jesus, you Nazarene? Have you come to destroy us? I know you who you are: the Holy One of God!" [25] Jesus rebuked him, saying, *"Be quiet, and come out of him!"* [26] The unclean spirit, convulsing him and crying with a loud voice, came out of him. [27] They were all amazed, so that they questioned among themselves, saying, "What is this? A new teaching? For with authority he commands even the unclean spirits, and they obey him!" [28] The report of him went out immediately everywhere into all the region of Galilee and its surrounding area.

Jesus Heals Many People
• **Mark 1: 29-34 (Matthew 8: 14-17; Luke 4: 38-41)**

[29] Immediately, when they had come out of the synagogue, they came into the house of Simon and Andrew, with James and John. [30] Now Simon's wife's mother lay sick with a fever, and immediately they told him about her. [31] He came and took her by the hand, and raised her up. The fever left her, and she served them. [32] At evening, when the sun had set, they brought to him all who were sick, and those who were possessed by demons. [33] All the city was gathered together at the door. [34] He healed many who were sick with various diseases, and cast out many demons. He didn't allow the demons to speak, because they knew him.

Spreading the Good News
- ### Mark 1: 35-39 (Matthew 4: 23-25; Luke 4: 42-44)

[35] Early in the morning, while it was still dark, he rose up and went out, and departed into a deserted place, and prayed there. [36] Simon and those who were with him followed after him; [37] and they found him, and told him, "Everyone is looking for you." [38] He said to them, *"Let's go elsewhere into the next towns, that I may preach there also, because I came out for this reason."* [39] He went into their synagogues throughout all Galilee, preaching and casting out demons.

Fishers of Men
- ### Luke 5: 1-11 (Matthew 4: 18-22; Mark 1: 16-20)

[1] Now it happened, while the multitude pressed on him and heard the word of God, that he was standing by the lake of Gennesaret. [2] He saw two boats standing by the lake, but the fishermen had gone out of them, and were washing their nets. [3] He entered into one of the boats, which was Simon's, and asked him to put out a little from the land. He sat down and taught the multitudes from the boat. [4] When he had finished speaking, he said to Simon, *"Put out into the deep, and let down your nets for a catch."* [5] Simon answered him, "Master, we worked all night, and took nothing; but at your word I will let down the net." [6] When they had done this, they caught a great multitude of fish, and their net was breaking. [7] They beckoned to their partners in the other boat, that they should come and help them. They came, and filled both boats, so that they began to sink. [8] But Simon Peter, when he saw it, fell down at Jesus' knees, saying, "Depart from me, for I am a sinful man, Lord." [9] For he was amazed, and all who were with him, at the catch of fish which they had caught; [10] and so also were James and John, sons of Zebedee, who were partners with Simon. Jesus said to Simon, *"Don't be afraid. From now on you will be catching people alive."* [11] When they had brought their boats to land, they left everything, and followed him.

Jesus Heals a Man with Leprosy
- ### Mark 1: 40-45 (Matthew 8: 1-4; Luke 5: 12-16)

[40] A leper came to him, begging him, kneeling down to him, and saying to him, "If you want to, you can make me clean." [41] Being

moved with compassion, he stretched out his hand, and touched him, and said to him, *"I want to. Be made clean."* [42] When he had said this, immediately the leprosy departed from him, and he was made clean. [43] He strictly warned him, and immediately sent him out, [44] and said to him, *"See you say nothing to anybody, but go show yourself to the priest, and offer for your cleansing the things which Moses commanded, for a testimony to them."* [45] But he went out, and began to proclaim it much, and to spread about the matter, so that Jesus could no more openly enter into a city, but was outside in desert places: and they came to him from everywhere.

Jesus Heals a Paralyzed Man
   • **Mark 2: 1-12 (Matthew 9: 1-8; Luke 5: 17-26)**
[1] When he entered again into Capernaum after some days, it was heard that he was in the house. [2] Immediately many were gathered together, so that there was no more room, not even around the door; and he spoke the word to them. [3] Four people came, carrying a paralytic to him. [4] When they could not come near to him for the crowd, they removed the roof where he was. When they had broken it up, they let down the mat that the paralytic was lying on. [5] Jesus, seeing their faith, said to the paralytic, *"Son, your sins are forgiven you."*
[6] But there were some of the scribes sitting there, and reasoning in their hearts, [7] "Why does this man speak blasphemies like that? Who can forgive sins but God alone?" [8] Immediately Jesus, perceiving in his spirit that they so reasoned within themselves, said to them, *"Why do you reason these things in your hearts? [9] Which is easier, to tell the paralytic, 'Your sins are forgiven;' or to say, 'Arise, and take up your bed, and walk?' [10] But that you may know that the Son of Man has authority on earth to forgive sins"* — he said to the paralytic — [11] *"I tell you, arise, take up your mat, and go to your house."* [12] He arose, and immediately took up the mat, and went out in front of them all; so that they were all amazed, and glorified God, saying, "We never saw anything like this!"

Jesus Calls Matthew
- **Matthew 9: 9-13 (Mark 2: 13-17; Luke 5: 27-32)**

⁹ As Jesus passed by from there, he saw a man called Matthew sitting at the tax collection office. He said to him, *"Follow me."* He got up and followed him. ¹⁰ It happened as he sat in the house, behold, many tax collectors and sinners came and sat down with Jesus and his disciples. ¹¹ When the Pharisees saw it, they said to his disciples, "Why does your teacher eat with tax collectors and sinners?" ¹² When Jesus heard it, he said to them, *"Those who are healthy have no need for a physician, but those who are sick do. ¹³ But you go and learn what this means: 'I desire mercy, and not sacrifice,' for I came not to call the righteous, but sinners to repentance."*

Jesus Questioned About Fasting
- **Mark 2: 18-22 (Matthew 9: 14-17; Luke 5: 33-39)**

¹⁸ John's disciples and the Pharisees were fasting, and they came and asked him, "Why do John's disciples and the disciples of the Pharisees fast, but your disciples don't fast?" ¹⁹ Jesus said to them, *"Can the groomsmen fast while the bridegroom is with them? As long as they have the bridegroom with them, they can't fast. ²⁰ But the days will come when the bridegroom will be taken away from them, and then will they fast in that day. ²¹ No one sews a piece of unshrunk cloth on an old garment, or else the patch shrinks and the new tears away from the old, and a worse hole is made. ²² No one puts new wine into old wineskins, or else the new wine will burst the skins, and the wine pours out, and the skins will be destroyed; but they put new wine into fresh wineskins."*

At the Healing Pool
- **John 5: 1-15**

¹ After these things, there was a feast of the Jews, and Jesus went up to Jerusalem. ² Now in Jerusalem by the sheep gate, there is a pool, which is called in Hebrew, "Bethesda," having five porches. ³ In these lay a great multitude of those who were sick, blind, lame, or paralyzed, waiting for the moving of the water; ⁴ for an angel went down at certain times into the pool, and stirred up the water. Whoever stepped in first after the stirring of the water was made

whole of whatever disease he had. [5] A certain man was there, who had been sick for thirty-eight years. [6] When Jesus saw him lying there, and knew that he had been sick for a long time, he asked him, *"Do you want to be made well?"* [7] The sick man answered him, "Sir, I have no one to put me into the pool when the water is stirred up, but while I'm coming, another steps down before me." [8] Jesus said to him, *"Arise, take up your mat, and walk."* [9] Immediately, the man was made well, and took up his mat and walked. Now it was the Sabbath on that day. [10] So the Jews said to him who was cured, "It is the Sabbath. It is not lawful for you to carry the mat." [11] He answered them, "He who made me well, the same said to me, *'Take up your mat, and walk.'*" [12] Then they asked him, "Who is the man who said to you, *'Take up your mat, and walk'*?" [13] But he who was healed didn't know who it was, for Jesus had withdrawn, a crowd being in the place. [14] Afterward Jesus found him in the temple, and said to him, *"Behold, you are made well. Sin no more, so that nothing worse happens to you."* [15] The man went away, and told the Jews that it was Jesus who had made him well.

Life Through the Son
- **John 5: 16-30**

[16] For this cause the Jews persecuted Jesus, and sought to kill him, because he did these things on the Sabbath. [17] But Jesus answered them, *"My Father is still working, so I am working, too."* [18] For this cause therefore the Jews sought all the more to kill him, because he not only broke the Sabbath, but also called God his own Father, making himself equal with God. [19] Jesus therefore answered them, *"Most certainly, I tell you, the Son can do nothing of himself, but what he sees the Father doing. For whatever things he does, these the Son also does likewise. [20] For the Father has affection for the Son, and shows him all things that he himself does. He will show him greater works than these, that you may marvel. [21] For as the Father raises the dead and gives them life, even so the Son also gives life to whom he desires. [22] For the Father judges no one, but he has given all judgment to the Son, [23] that all may honor the Son, even as they honor the Father. He who doesn't honor the Son doesn't honor the Father who sent him. [24] "Most certainly I tell you, he who*

hears my word, and believes him who sent me, has eternal life, and doesn't come into judgment, but has passed out of death into life. [25] Most certainly, I tell you, the hour comes, and now is, when the dead will hear the Son of God's voice; and those who hear will live. [26] For as the Father has life in himself, even so he gave to the Son also to have life in himself. [27] He also gave him authority to execute judgment, because he is a son of man. [28] Don't marvel at this, for the hour comes, in which all that are in the tombs will hear his voice, [29] and will come out; those who have done good, to the resurrection of life; and those who have done evil, to the resurrection of judgment. [30] I can of myself do nothing. As I hear, I judge, and my judgment is righteous; because I don't seek my own will, but the will of my Father who sent me.

Testimonies About Jesus
- **John 5: 31-47**

[31] "If I testify about myself, my witness is not valid. [32] It is another who testifies about me. I know that the testimony which he testifies about me is true. [33] You have sent to John, and he has testified to the truth. [34] But the testimony which I receive is not from man. However, I say these things that you may be saved. [35] He was the burning and shining lamp, and you were willing to rejoice for a while in his light. [36] But the testimony which I have is greater than that of John, for the works which the Father gave me to accomplish, the very works that I do, testify about me, that the Father has sent me. [37] The Father himself, who sent me, has testified about me. You have neither heard his voice at any time, nor seen his form. [38] You don't have his word living in you; because you don't believe him whom he sent. [39] "You search the Scriptures, because you think that in them you have eternal life; and these are they which testify about me. [40] Yet you will not come to me, that you may have life. [41] I don't receive glory from men. [42] But I know you, that you don't have God's love in yourselves. [43] I have come in my Father's name, and you don't receive me. If another comes in his own name, you will receive him. [44] How can you believe, who receive glory from one another, and you don't seek the glory that comes from the only God? [45] "Don't think that I will accuse you to the Father. There is one who accuses you,

even Moses, on whom you have set your hope. ⁴⁶ For if you believed Moses, you would believe me; for he wrote about me. ⁴⁷ But if you don't believe his writings, how will you believe my words?"

Lord of the Sabbath
• **Matthew 12: 1-14 (Mark 2: 23-28 & 3: 1-6; Luke 6: 1-11)**
¹ At that time, Jesus went on the Sabbath day through the grain fields. His disciples were hungry and began to pluck heads of grain and to eat. ² But the Pharisees, when they saw it, said to him, "Behold, your disciples do what is not lawful to do on the Sabbath." ³ But he said to them, *"Haven't you read what David did, when he was hungry, and those who were with him; ⁴ how he entered into God's house, and ate the show bread, which was not lawful for him to eat, neither for those who were with him, but only for the priests? ⁵ Or have you not read in the law, that on the Sabbath day, the priests in the temple profane the Sabbath, and are guiltless? ⁶ But I tell you that one greater than the temple is here. ⁷ But if you had known what this means, 'I desire mercy, and not sacrifice,' you would not have condemned the guiltless. ⁸ For the Son of Man is Lord of the Sabbath."*
⁹ He departed there, and went into their synagogue. ¹⁰ And behold there was a man with a withered hand. They asked him, "Is it lawful to heal on the Sabbath day?" that they might accuse him. ¹¹ He said to them, *"What man is there among you, who has one sheep, and if this one falls into a pit on the Sabbath day, won't he grab on to it, and lift it out? ¹² Of how much more value then is a man than a sheep! Therefore it is lawful to do good on the Sabbath day."* ¹³ Then he told the man, *"Stretch out your hand."* He stretched it out; and it was restored whole, just like the other. ¹⁴ But the Pharisees went out, and conspired against him, how they might destroy him.

God's Chosen Servant
• **Matthew 12: 15-21 (Mark 3: 7-12)**
¹⁵ Jesus, perceiving that, withdrew from there. Great multitudes followed him; and he healed them all, ¹⁶ and commanded them that they should not make him known: ¹⁷ that it might be fulfilled which was spoken through Isaiah the prophet, saying, ¹⁸ "Behold, my servant whom I have chosen; my beloved in whom my soul is well pleased:

I will put my Spirit on him. He will proclaim justice to the nations. [19] He will not strive, nor shout; neither will anyone hear his voice in the streets. [20] He won't break a bruised reed. He won't quench a smoking flax, until he leads justice to victory. [21] In his name, the nations will hope."

The Beatitudes
  * **Matthew 5: 1-12 (Luke 6: 17-26)**

[1] Seeing the multitudes, he went up onto the mountain. When he had sat down, his disciples came to him. [2] He opened his mouth and taught them, saying, [3] *"Blessed are the poor in spirit, for theirs is the Kingdom of Heaven. [4] Blessed are those who mourn, for they shall be comforted. [5] Blessed are the gentle, for they shall inherit the earth. [6] Blessed are those who hunger and thirst after righteousness, for they shall be filled. [7] Blessed are the merciful, for they shall obtain mercy. [8] Blessed are the pure in heart, for they shall see God. [9] Blessed are the peacemakers, for they shall be called children of God. [10] Blessed are those who have been persecuted for righteousness' sake, for theirs is the Kingdom of Heaven. [11] "Blessed are you when people reproach you, persecute you, and say all kinds of evil against you falsely, for my sake. [12] Rejoice, and be exceedingly glad, for great is your reward in heaven. For that is how they persecuted the prophets who were before you.*

Salt and Light
  * **Matthew 5: 13-16**

[13] *"You are the salt of the earth, but if the salt has lost its flavor, with what will it be salted? It is then good for nothing, but to be cast out and trodden under the feet of men. [14] You are the light of the world. A city located on a hill can't be hidden. [15] Neither do you light a lamp, and put it under a measuring basket, but on a stand; and it shines to all who are in the house. [16] Even so, let your light shine before men; that they may see your good works, and glorify your Father who is in heaven.*

Fulfillment of the Law
- **Matthew 5: 17-20 (Luke 16: 16-17)**

[17] "Don't think that I came to destroy the law or the prophets. I didn't come to destroy, but to fulfill. [18] For most certainly, I tell you, until heaven and earth pass away, not even one smallest letter or one tiny pen stroke shall in any way pass away from the law, until all things are accomplished. [19] Whoever, therefore, shall break one of these least commandments, and teach others to do so, shall be called least in the Kingdom of Heaven; but whoever shall do and teach them shall be called great in the Kingdom of Heaven. [20] For I tell you that unless your righteousness exceeds that of the scribes and Pharisees, there is no way you will enter into the Kingdom of Heaven.

Murder
- **Matthew 5: 21-26**

[21] "You have heard that it was said to the ancient ones, 'You shall not murder;' and 'Whoever shall murder shall be in danger of the judgment.' [22] But I tell you, that everyone who is angry with his brother without a cause shall be in danger of the judgment; and whoever shall say to his brother, 'Raca!' shall be in danger of the council; and whoever shall say, 'You fool!' shall be in danger of the fire of Gehenna. [23] "If therefore you are offering your gift at the altar, and there remember that your brother has anything against you, [24] leave your gift there before the altar, and go your way. First be reconciled to your brother, and then come and offer your gift. [25] Agree with your adversary quickly, while you are with him on the way; lest perhaps the prosecutor deliver you to the judge, and the judge deliver you to the officer, and you be cast into prison. [26] Most certainly I tell you, you shall by no means get out of there, until you have paid the last penny.

Adultery
- **Matthew 5: 27-30**

[27] "You have heard that it was said, 'You shall not commit adultery;' [28] but I tell you that everyone who gazes at a woman to lust after her has committed adultery with her already in his heart. [29] If your right eye causes you to stumble, pluck it out and throw it away

from you. For it is more profitable for you that one of your members should perish, than for your whole body to be cast into Gehenna. [30] *If your right hand causes you to stumble, cut it off, and throw it away from you. For it is more profitable for you that one of your members should perish, than for your whole body to be cast into Gehenna.*

Divorce
- ### Matthew 5: 31-32 (Luke 16: 18)

[31] *"It was also said, 'Whoever shall put away his wife, let him give her a writing of divorce,'* [32] *but I tell you that whoever puts away his wife, except for the cause of sexual immorality, makes her an adulteress; and whoever marries her when she is put away commits adultery.*

Oaths
- ### Matthew 5: 33-37

[33] *"Again you have heard that it was said to them of old time, 'You shall not make false vows, but shall perform to the Lord your vows,'* [34] *but I tell you, don't swear at all: neither by heaven, for it is the throne of God;* [35] *nor by the earth, for it is the footstool of his feet; nor by Jerusalem, for it is the city of the great King.* [36] *Neither shall you swear by your head, for you can't make one hair white or black.* [37] *But let your 'Yes' be 'Yes' and your 'No' be 'No.' Whatever is more than these is of the evil one.*

Love Your Enemies
- ### Matthew 5: 38-48 (Luke 6: 27-30 & 32-36)

[38] *"You have heard that it was said, 'An eye for an eye, and a tooth for a tooth.'* [39] *But I tell you, don't resist him who is evil; but whoever strikes you on your right cheek, turn to him the other also.* [40] *If anyone sues you to take away your coat, let him have your cloak also.* [41] *Whoever compels you to go one mile, go with him two.* [42] *Give to him who asks you, and don't turn away him who desires to borrow from you.* [43] *"You have heard that it was said, 'You shall love your neighbor, and hate your enemy.'* [44] *But I tell you, love your enemies, bless those who curse you, do good to those who hate you, and pray for those who mistreat you and persecute you,* [45] *that you*

may be children of your Father who is in heaven. For he makes his sun to rise on the evil and the good, and sends rain on the just and the unjust. [46] *For if you love those who love you, what reward do you have? Don't even the tax collectors do the same?* [47] *If you only greet your friends, what more do you do than others? Don't even the tax collectors do the same?* [48] *Therefore you shall be perfect, just as your Father in heaven is perfect.*

Giving to the Needy
  * **Matthew 6: 1-4**

[1] *"Be careful that you don't do your charitable giving before men, to be seen by them, or else you have no reward from your Father who is in heaven.* [2] *Therefore when you do merciful deeds, don't sound a trumpet before yourself, as the hypocrites do in the synagogues and in the streets, that they may get glory from men. Most certainly I tell you, they have received their reward.* [3] *But when you do merciful deeds, don't let your left hand know what your right hand does,* [4] *so that your merciful deeds may be in secret, then your Father who sees in secret will reward you openly.*

Fasting
  * **Matthew 6: 16-18**

[16] *"Moreover when you fast, don't be like the hypocrites, with sad faces. For they disfigure their faces, that they may be seen by men to be fasting. Most certainly I tell you, they have received their reward.* [17] *But you, when you fast, anoint your head, and wash your face;* [18] *so that you are not seen by men to be fasting, but by your Father who is in secret, and your Father, who sees in secret, will reward you.*

Treasures in Heaven
  * **Matthew 6: 19-24**

[19] *"Don't lay up treasures for yourselves on the earth, where moth and rust consume, and where thieves break through and steal;* [20] *but lay up for yourselves treasures in heaven, where neither moth nor rust consume, and where thieves don't break through and steal;* [21] *for where your treasure is, there your heart will be also.* [22] *"The lamp of the body is the eye. If therefore your eye is sound, your whole body*

will be full of light. ²³ But if your eye is evil, your whole body will be full of darkness. If therefore the light that is in you is darkness, how great is the darkness! ²⁴ "No one can serve two masters, for either he will hate the one and love the other; or else he will be devoted to one and despise the other. You can't serve both God and Mammon.

Do not Worry
   ● **Matthew 6: 25-34 (Luke 12: 22-34)**

²⁵ Therefore I tell you, don't be anxious for your life: what you will eat, or what you will drink; nor yet for your body, what you will wear. Isn't life more than food, and the body more than clothing? ²⁶ See the birds of the sky, that they don't sow, neither do they reap, nor gather into barns. Your heavenly Father feeds them. Aren't you of much more value than they? ²⁷ "Which of you, by being anxious, can add one moment to his lifespan? ²⁸ Why are you anxious about clothing? Consider the lilies of the field, how they grow. They don't toil, neither do they spin, ²⁹ yet I tell you that even Solomon in all his glory was not dressed like one of these. ³⁰ But if God so clothes the grass of the field, which today exists, and tomorrow is thrown into the oven, won't he much more clothe you, you of little faith? ³¹ "Therefore don't be anxious, saying, 'What will we eat?', 'What will we drink?' or, 'With what will we be clothed?' ³² For the Gentiles seek after all these things; for your heavenly Father knows that you need all these things. ³³ But seek first God's Kingdom, and his righteousness; and all these things will be given to you as well. ³⁴ Therefore don't be anxious for tomorrow, for tomorrow will be anxious for itself. Each day's own evil is sufficient.

Judging Others
   ● **Matthew 7: 1-6 (Luke 6: 37-42)**

¹ "Don't judge, so that you won't be judged. ² For with whatever judgment you judge, you will be judged; and with whatever measure you measure, it will be measured to you. ³ Why do you see the speck that is in your brother's eye, but don't consider the beam that is in your own eye? ⁴ Or how will you tell your brother, 'Let me remove the speck from your eye;' and behold, the beam is in your own eye? ⁵ You hypocrite! First remove the beam out of your own eye, and then you can see clearly to remove the speck out of your brother's eye. [6] *"Don't give that which is holy to the dogs, neither throw your pearls before the pigs, lest perhaps they trample them under their feet, and turn and tear you to pieces.*

The Golden Rule
- **Matthew 7: 12 (Luke 6: 31)**

[12] *Therefore whatever you desire for men to do to you, you shall also do to them; for this is the law and the prophets.*

Narrow and Wide Gates
- **Matthew 7: 13-14**

[13] *"Enter in by the narrow gate; for wide is the gate and broad is the way that leads to destruction, and many are those who enter in by it.* [14] *How narrow is the gate, and restricted is the way that leads to life! Few are those who find it.*

A Tree and its Fruit
- **Matthew 7: 15-20 (Luke 6: 43-45)**

[15] *"Beware of false prophets, who come to you in sheep's clothing, but inwardly are ravening wolves.* [16] *By their fruits you will know them. Do you gather grapes from thorns, or figs from thistles?* [17] *Even so, every good tree produces good fruit; but the corrupt tree produces evil fruit.* [18] *A good tree can't produce evil fruit, neither can a corrupt tree produce good fruit.* [19] *Every tree that doesn't grow good fruit is cut down, and thrown into the fire.* [20] *Therefore by their fruits you will know them.*

A Solid Foundation
- **Matthew 7: 21-29 (Luke 6: 46-49)**

[21] *Not everyone who says to me, 'Lord, Lord,' will enter into the Kingdom of Heaven; but he who does the will of my Father who is in heaven.* [22] *Many will tell me in that day, 'Lord, Lord, didn't we prophesy in your name, in your name cast out demons, and in your name do many mighty works?'* [23] *Then I will tell them, 'I never knew you. Depart from me, you who work iniquity.'* [24] *"Everyone therefore who hears these words of mine, and does them, I will liken him to*

a wise man, who built his house on a rock. ²⁵ *The rain came down, the floods came, and the winds blew, and beat on that house; and it didn't fall, for it was founded on the rock.* ²⁶ *Everyone who hears these words of mine, and doesn't do them will be like a foolish man, who built his house on the sand.* ²⁷ *The rain came down, the floods came, and the winds blew, and beat on that house; and it fell—and great was its fall."* ²⁸ It happened, when Jesus had finished saying these things, that the multitudes were astonished at his teaching, ²⁹ for he taught them with authority, and not like the scribes.

Faith of an Army Officer
- **Matthew 8: 5-13 (Luke 7: 1-10)**

⁵ When he came into Capernaum, a centurion came to him, asking him, ⁶ and saying, "Lord, my servant lies in the house paralyzed, grievously tormented." ⁷ Jesus said to him, *"I will come and heal him."* ⁸ The centurion answered, "Lord, I'm not worthy for you to come under my roof. Just say the word, and my servant will be healed. ⁹ For I am also a man under authority, having under myself soldiers. I tell this one, 'Go,' and he goes; and tell another, 'Come,' and he comes; and tell my servant, 'Do this,' and he does it." ¹⁰ When Jesus heard it, he marveled, and said to those who followed, *"Most certainly I tell you, I haven't found so great a faith, not even in Israel.* ¹¹ *I tell you that many will come from the east and the west, and will sit down with Abraham, Isaac, and Jacob in the Kingdom of Heaven,* ¹² *but the children of the Kingdom will be thrown out into the outer darkness. There will be weeping and gnashing of teeth."* ¹³ Jesus said to the centurion, *"Go your way. Let it be done for you as you have believed."* His servant was healed in that hour.

Jesus Raises a Widow's Son
- **Luke 7: 11-17**

¹¹ It happened soon afterwards, that he went to a city called Nain. Many of his disciples, along with a great multitude, went with him. ¹² Now when he drew near to the gate of the city, behold, one who was dead was carried out, the only son of his mother, and she was a widow. Many people of the city were with her. ¹³ When the Lord saw her, he had compassion on her, and said to her, *"Don't cry."* ¹⁴

He came near and touched the coffin, and the bearers stood still. He said, *"Young man, I tell you, arise!"* [15] He who was dead sat up, and began to speak. And he gave him to his mother. [16] Fear took hold of all, and they glorified God, saying, "A great prophet has arisen among us!" and, "God has visited his people!" [17] This report went out concerning him in the whole of Judea, and in all the surrounding region.

Jesus and John the Baptist
- **Matthew 11: 1-19 (Luke 7: 18-35)**

[1] It happened that when Jesus had finished directing his twelve disciples, he departed from there to teach and preach in their cities. [2] Now when John heard in the prison the works of Christ, he sent two of his disciples [3] and said to him, "Are you he who comes, or should we look for another?" [4] Jesus answered them, *"Go and tell John the things which you hear and see: [5] the blind receive their sight, the lame walk, the lepers are cleansed, the deaf hear, the dead are raised up, and the poor have good news preached to them. [6] Blessed is he who finds no occasion for stumbling in me."* [7] As these went their way, Jesus began to say to the multitudes concerning John, *"What did you go out into the wilderness to see? A reed shaken by the wind? [8] But what did you go out to see? A man in soft clothing? Behold, those who wear soft clothing are in king's houses. [9] But why did you go out? To see a prophet? Yes, I tell you, and much more than a prophet. [10] For this is he, of whom it is written, 'Behold, I send my messenger before your face, who will prepare your way before you.' [11] Most certainly I tell you, among those who are born of women there has not arisen anyone greater than John the Baptizer; yet he who is least in the Kingdom of Heaven is greater than he. [12] From the days of John the Baptizer until now, the Kingdom of Heaven suffers violence, and the violent take it by force. [13] For all the prophets and the law prophesied until John. [14] If you are willing to receive it, this is Elijah, who is to come. [15] He who has ears to hear, let him hear. [16] "But to what shall I compare this generation? It is like children sitting in the marketplaces, who call to their companions [17] and say, 'We played the flute for you, and you didn't dance. We mourned for you, and you didn't lament.' [18] For John came neither eating nor*

drinking, and they say, 'He has a demon.' [19] The Son of Man came eating and drinking, and they say, 'Behold, a gluttonous man and a drunkard, a friend of tax collectors and sinners!' But wisdom is justified by her children."

Jesus Anointed by a Sinful Woman
* **Luke 7: 36-50**

[36] One of the Pharisees invited him to eat with him. He entered into the Pharisee's house, and sat at the table. [37] Behold, a woman in the city who was a sinner, when she knew that he was reclining in the Pharisee's house, she brought an alabaster jar of ointment. [38] Standing behind at his feet weeping, she began to wet his feet with her tears, and she wiped them with the hair of her head, kissed his feet, and anointed them with the ointment. [39] Now when the Pharisee who had invited him saw it, he said to himself, "This man, if he were a prophet, would have perceived who and what kind of woman this is who touches him, that she is a sinner." [40] Jesus answered him, *"Simon, I have something to tell you."* He said, "Teacher, say on." [41] *"A certain lender had two debtors. The one owed five hundred denarii, and the other fifty. [42] When they couldn't pay, he forgave them both. Which of them therefore will love him most?"* [43] Simon answered, "He, I suppose, to whom he forgave the most." He said to him, *"You have judged correctly."* [44] Turning to the woman, he said to Simon, *"Do you see this woman? I entered into your house, and you gave me no water for my feet, but she has wet my feet with her tears, and wiped them with the hair of her head. [45] You gave me no kiss, but she, since the time I came in, has not ceased to kiss my feet. [46] You didn't anoint my head with oil, but she has anointed my feet with ointment. [47] Therefore I tell you, her sins, which are many, are forgiven, for she loved much. But to whom little is forgiven, the same loves little."* [48] He said to her, *"Your sins are forgiven."* [49] Those who sat at the table with him began to say to themselves, "Who is this who even forgives sins?" [50] He said to the woman, *"Your faith has saved you. Go in peace."*

Followers of Jesus
- ### Luke 8: 1-3

[1] It happened soon afterwards, that he went about through cities and villages, preaching and bringing the good news of the Kingdom of God. With him were the twelve, [2] and certain women who had been healed of evil spirits and infirmities: Mary who was called Magdalene, from whom seven demons had gone out; [3] and Joanna, the wife of Chuzas, Herod's steward; Susanna; and many others; who served them from their possessions.

The Sower
- ### Matthew 13: 1-23 (Mark 4: 1-20; Luke 8: 4-15)

[1] On that day Jesus went out of the house, and sat by the seaside. [2] Great multitudes gathered to him, so that he entered into a boat, and sat, and all the multitude stood on the beach. [3] He spoke to them many things in parables, saying, *"Behold, a farmer went out to sow.* [4] *As he sowed, some seeds fell by the roadside, and the birds came and devoured them.* [5] *Others fell on rocky ground, where they didn't have much soil, and immediately they sprang up, because they had no depth of earth.* [6] *When the sun had risen, they were scorched. Because they had no root, they withered away.* [7] *Others fell among thorns. The thorns grew up and choked them.* [8] *Others fell on good soil, and yielded fruit: some one hundred times as much, some sixty, and some thirty.* [9] *He who has ears to hear, let him hear."* [10] The disciples came, and said to him, "Why do you speak to them in parables?" [11] He answered them, *"To you it is given to know the mysteries of the Kingdom of Heaven, but it is not given to them.* [12] *For whoever has, to him will be given, and he will have abundance, but whoever doesn't have, from him will be taken away even that which he has.* [13] *Therefore I speak to them in parables, because seeing they don't see, and hearing, they don't hear, neither do they understand.* [14] *In them the prophecy of Isaiah is fulfilled, which says, 'By hearing you will hear, and will in no way understand; Seeing you will see, and will in no way perceive:* [15] *for this people's heart has grown callous, their ears are dull of hearing, they have closed their eyes; or else perhaps they might perceive with their eyes, hear with their ears, understand with their heart, and should turn again; and*

I would heal them.' [16] *"But blessed are your eyes, for they see; and your ears, for they hear.* [17] *For most certainly I tell you that many prophets and righteous men desired to see the things which you see, and didn't see them; and to hear the things which you hear, and didn't hear them.* [18] *"Hear, then, the parable of the farmer.* [19] *When anyone hears the word of the Kingdom, and doesn't understand it, the evil one comes, and snatches away that which has been sown in his heart. This is what was sown by the roadside.* [20] *What was sown on the rocky places, this is he who hears the word, and immediately with joy receives it;* [21] *yet he has no root in himself, but endures for a while. When oppression or persecution arises because of the word, immediately he stumbles.* [22] *What was sown among the thorns, this is he who hears the word, but the cares of this age and the deceitfulness of riches choke the word, and he becomes unfruitful.* [23] *What was sown on the good ground, this is he who hears the word, and understands it, who most certainly bears fruit, and brings forth, some one hundred times as much, some sixty, and some thirty."*

The Weeds
• Matthew 13: 24-30 & 36-43

[24] He set another parable before them, saying, *"The Kingdom of Heaven is like a man who sowed good seed in his field,* [25] *but while people slept, his enemy came and sowed darnel weeds also among the wheat, and went away.* [26] *But when the blade sprang up and brought forth fruit, then the darnel weeds appeared also.* [27] *The servants of the householder came and said to him, 'Sir, didn't you sow good seed in your field? Where did this darnel come from?'* [28] *"He said to them, 'An enemy has done this.' "The servants asked him, 'Do you want us to go and gather them up?'* [29] *"But he said, 'No, lest perhaps while you gather up the darnel weeds, you root up the wheat with them.* [30] *Let both grow together until the harvest, and in the harvest time I will tell the reapers, "First, gather up the darnel weeds, and bind them in bundles to burn them; but gather the wheat into my barn." ' "*

[36] Then Jesus sent the multitudes away, and went into the house. His disciples came to him, saying, "Explain to us the parable of the

darnel weeds of the field." [37] He answered them, *"He who sows the good seed is the Son of Man, [38] the field is the world; and the good seed, these are the children of the Kingdom; and the darnel weeds are the children of the evil one. [39] The enemy who sowed them is the devil. The harvest is the end of the age, and the reapers are angels. [40] As therefore the darnel weeds are gathered up and burned with fire; so will it be at the end of this age. [41] The Son of Man will send out his angels, and they will gather out of his Kingdom all things that cause stumbling, and those who do iniquity, [42] and will cast them into the furnace of fire. There will be weeping and the gnashing of teeth. [43] Then the righteous will shine forth like the sun in the Kingdom of their Father. He who has ears to hear, let him hear.*

Lamp on the Stand
• Mark 4: 21-25 (Luke 8: 16-18)
[21] He said to them, *"Is the lamp brought to be put under a basket or under a bed? Isn't it put on a stand? [22] For there is nothing hidden, except that it should be made known; neither was anything made secret, but that it should come to light. [23] If any man has ears to hear, let him hear."* [24] He said to them, *"Take heed what you hear. With whatever measure you measure, it will be measured to you, and more will be given to you who hear. [25] For whoever has, to him will more be given, and he who doesn't have, even that which he has will be taken away from him."*

Jesus' Mother and Brothers
• Matthew 12: 46-50 (Mark 3: 31-35; Luke 8: 19-21)
[46] While he was yet speaking to the multitudes, behold, his mother and his brothers stood outside, seeking to speak to him. [47] One said to him, "Behold, your mother and your brothers stand outside, seeking to speak to you." [48] But he answered him who spoke to him, *"Who is my mother? Who are my brothers?"* [49] He stretched out his hand towards his disciples, and said, *"Behold, my mother and my brothers! [50] For whoever does the will of my Father who is in heaven, he is my brother, and sister, and mother."*

The Growing Seed
- **Mark 4: 26-29**

26 He said, *"The Kingdom of God is as if a man should cast seed on the earth,* 27 *and should sleep and rise night and day, and the seed should spring up and grow, he doesn't know how.* 28 *For the earth bears fruit: first the blade, then the ear, then the full grain in the ear.* 29 *But when the fruit is ripe, immediately he puts forth the sickle, because the harvest has come."*

The Mustard Seed
- **Matthew 13: 31-32 (Mark 4: 30-32; Luke 13: 18-19)**

31 He set another parable before them, saying, *"The Kingdom of Heaven is like a grain of mustard seed, which a man took, and sowed in his field;* 32 *which indeed is smaller than all seeds. But when it is grown, it is greater than the herbs, and becomes a tree, so that the birds of the air come and lodge in its branches."*

The Yeast
- **Luke 13: 20-21 (Matthew 13: 33)**

20 Again he said, *"To what shall I compare the Kingdom of God?* 21 *It is like yeast, which a woman took and hid in three measures of flour, until it was all leavened."*

Speaking in Parables
- **Matthew 13: 34-35 (Mark 4: 33-34)**

34 Jesus spoke all these things in parables to the multitudes; and without a parable, he didn't speak to them, 35 that it might be fulfilled which was spoken through the prophet, saying, "I will open my mouth in parables; I will utter things hidden from the foundation of the world."

The Hidden Treasure
- **Matthew 13: 44**

[44] *"Again, the Kingdom of Heaven is like a treasure hidden in the field, which a man found, and hid. In his joy, he goes and sells all that he has, and buys that field.*

The Pearl
- **Matthew 13: 45-46**

[45] *"Again, the Kingdom of Heaven is like a man who is a merchant seeking fine pearls,* [46] *who having found one pearl of great price, he went and sold all that he had, and bought it.*

The Net
- **Matthew 13: 47-51**

[47] *"Again, the Kingdom of Heaven is like a dragnet, that was cast into the sea, and gathered some fish of every kind,* [48] *which, when it was filled, they drew up on the beach. They sat down, and gathered the good into containers, but the bad they threw away.* [49] *So will it be in the end of the world. The angels will come forth, and separate the wicked from among the righteous,* [50] *and will cast them into the furnace of fire. There will be the weeping and the gnashing of teeth."* [51] Jesus said to them, *"Have you understood all these things?"* They answered him, "Yes, Lord."

Knowledgeable Teachers
- **Matthew 13: 52-53**

[52] He said to them, *"Therefore every scribe who has been made a disciple in the Kingdom of Heaven is like a man who is a householder, who brings out of his treasure new and old things."* [53] It happened that when Jesus had finished these parables, he departed from there.

Jesus Calms the Storm
- **Mark 4: 35-41 (Matthew 8: 23-27; Luke 8: 22-25)**

[35] On that day, when evening had come, he said to them, *"Let's go over to the other side."* [36] Leaving the multitude, they took him with them, even as he was, in the boat. Other small boats were also with him. [37] A big wind storm arose, and the waves beat into the

boat, so much that the boat was already filled. [38] He himself was in the stern, asleep on the cushion, and they woke him up, and told him, "Teacher, don't you care that we are dying?" [39] He awoke, and rebuked the wind, and said to the sea, *"Peace! Be still!"* The wind ceased, and there was a great calm. [40] He said to them, *"Why are you so afraid? How is it that you have no faith?"* [41] They were greatly afraid, and said to one another, "Who then is this, that even the wind and the sea obey him?"

Jesus Heals a Demon-Possessed Man
- **Mark 5: 1-20 (Matthew 8: 28-34; Luke 8: 26-39)**

[1] They came to the other side of the sea, into the country of the Gadarenes. [2] When he had come out of the boat, immediately a man with an unclean spirit met him out of the tombs. [3] He lived in the tombs. Nobody could bind him any more, not even with chains, [4] because he had been often bound with fetters and chains, and the chains had been torn apart by him, and the fetters broken in pieces. Nobody had the strength to tame him. [5] Always, night and day, in the tombs and in the mountains, he was crying out, and cutting himself with stones. [6] When he saw Jesus from afar, he ran and bowed down to him, [7] and crying out with a loud voice, he said, "What have I to do with you, Jesus, you Son of the Most High God? I adjure you by God, don't torment me." [8] For he said to him, *"Come out of the man, you unclean spirit!"* [9] He asked him, *"What is your name?"* He said to him, "My name is Legion, for we are many." [10] He begged him much that he would not send them away out of the country. [11] Now on the mountainside there was a great herd of pigs feeding. [12] All the demons begged him, saying, "Send us into the pigs, that we may enter into them." [13] At once Jesus gave them permission. The unclean spirits came out and entered into the pigs. The herd of about two thousand rushed down the steep bank into the sea, and they were drowned in the sea. [14] Those who fed them fled, and told it in the city and in the country. The people came to see what it was that had happened. [15] They came to Jesus, and saw him who had been possessed by demons sitting, clothed, and in his right mind, even him who had the legion; and they were afraid. [16] Those who saw it declared to them how it happened to him who was possessed by demons, and about

the pigs. [17] They began to beg him to depart from their region. [18] As he was entering into the boat, he who had been possessed by demons begged him that he might be with him. [19] He didn't allow him, but said to him, *"Go to your house, to your friends, and tell them what great things the Lord has done for you, and how he had mercy on you."* [20] He went his way, and began to proclaim in Decapolis how Jesus had done great things for him, and everyone marveled.

A Dead Girl
- **Mark 5: 21-24 & 35-43 (Matthew 9: 18-19 & 23-26; Luke 8: 40-42 & 49-56)**

[21] When Jesus had crossed back over in the boat to the other side, a great multitude was gathered to him; and he was by the sea. [22] Behold, one of the rulers of the synagogue, Jairus by name, came; and seeing him, he fell at his feet, [23] and begged him much, saying, "My little daughter is at the point of death. Please come and lay your hands on her, that she may be made healthy, and live." [24] He went with him, and a great multitude followed him, and they pressed upon him on all sides.

[35] While he was still speaking, people came from the synagogue ruler's house saying, "Your daughter is dead. Why bother the Teacher any more?" [36] But Jesus, when he heard the message spoken, immediately said to the ruler of the synagogue, *"Don't be afraid, only believe."* [37] He allowed no one to follow him, except Peter, James, and John the brother of James. [38] He came to the synagogue ruler's house, and he saw an uproar, weeping, and great wailing. [39] When he had entered in, he said to them, *"Why do you make an uproar and weep? The child is not dead, but is asleep."* [40] They ridiculed him. But he, having put them all out, took the father of the child, her mother, and those who were with him, and went in where the child was lying. [41] Taking the child by the hand, he said to her, *"Talitha cumi!"* which means, being interpreted, *"Girl, I tell you, get up!"* [42] Immediately the girl rose up and walked, for she was twelve years old. They were amazed with great amazement. [43] He strictly ordered them that no one should know this, and commanded that something should be given to her to eat.

A Sick Woman
- **Mark 5: 25-34 (Matthew 9: 20-22; Luke 8: 43-48)**

[25] A certain woman, who had an issue of blood for twelve years, [26] and had suffered many things by many physicians, and had spent all that she had, and was no better, but rather grew worse, [27] having heard the things concerning Jesus, came up behind him in the crowd, and touched his clothes. [28] For she said, "If I just touch his clothes, I will be made well." [29] Immediately the flow of her blood was dried up, and she felt in her body that she was healed of her affliction. [30] Immediately Jesus, perceiving in himself that the power had gone out from him, turned around in the crowd, and asked, *"Who touched my clothes?"* [31] His disciples said to him, "You see the multitude pressing against you, and you say, 'Who touched me?'" [32] He looked around to see her who had done this thing. [33] But the woman, fearing and trembling, knowing what had been done to her, came and fell down before him, and told him all the truth. [34] He said to her, *"Daughter, your faith has made you well. Go in peace, and be cured of your disease."*

The Blind and Mute are Healed
- **Matthew 9: 27-34**

[27] As Jesus passed by from there, two blind men followed him, calling out and saying, "Have mercy on us, son of David!" [28] When he had come into the house, the blind men came to him. Jesus said to them, *"Do you believe that I am able to do this?"* They told him, "Yes, Lord." [29] Then he touched their eyes, saying, *"According to your faith be it done to you."* [30] Their eyes were opened. Jesus strictly commanded them, saying, *"See that no one knows about this."* [31] But they went out and spread abroad his fame in all that land. [32] As they went out, behold, a mute man who was demon possessed was brought to him. [33] When the demon was cast out, the mute man spoke. The multitudes marveled, saying, "Nothing like this has ever been seen in Israel!" [34] But the Pharisees said, "By the prince of the demons, he casts out demons."

The Workers are few
  • **Matthew 9: 35-38**

[35] Jesus went about all the cities and the villages, teaching in their synagogues, and preaching the Good News of the Kingdom, and healing every disease and every sickness among the people. [36] But when he saw the multitudes, he was moved with compassion for them, because they were harassed and scattered, like sheep without a shepherd. [37] Then he said to his disciples, *"The harvest indeed is plentiful, but the laborers are few. [38] Pray therefore that the Lord of the harvest will send out laborers into his harvest."*

Jesus Appoints the Twelve Disciples
  • **Matthew 10: 1-4 (Mark 3: 13-19; Luke 6: 12-16)**

[1] He called to himself his twelve disciples, and gave them authority over unclean spirits, to cast them out, and to heal every disease and every sickness. [2] Now the names of the twelve apostles are these. The first, Simon, who is called Peter; Andrew, his brother; James the son of Zebedee; John, his brother; [3] Philip; Bartholomew; Thomas; Matthew the tax collector; James the son of Alphaeus; Lebbaeus, who was also called Thaddaeus; [4] Simon the Canaanite; and Judas Iscariot, who also betrayed him.

Jesus Sends Out the Twelve Disciples
  • **Matthew 10: 5-42 (Mark 6: 6b-13; Luke 9: 1-6)**

[5] Jesus sent these twelve out, and commanded them, saying, *"Don't go among the Gentiles, and don't enter into any city of the Samaritans. [6] Rather, go to the lost sheep of the house of Israel. [7] As you go, preach, saying, 'The Kingdom of Heaven is at hand!' [8] Heal the sick, cleanse the lepers, and cast out demons. Freely you received, so freely give. [9] Don't take any gold, nor silver, nor brass in your money belts. [10] Take no bag for your journey, neither two coats, nor shoes, nor staff: for the laborer is worthy of his food. [11] Into whatever city or village you enter, find out who in it is worthy; and stay there until you go on. [12] As you enter into the household, greet it. [13] If the household is worthy, let your peace come on it, but if it isn't worthy, let your peace return to you. [14] Whoever doesn't receive you, nor hear your words, as you go out of that house or that city, shake off the*

dust from your feet. ¹⁵ Most certainly I tell you, it will be more toler-able for the land of Sodom and Gomorrah in the day of judgment than for that city. ¹⁶ "Behold, I send you out as sheep in the midst of wolves. Therefore be wise as serpents, and harmless as doves. ¹⁷ But beware of men: for they will deliver you up to councils, and in their synagogues they will scourge you. ¹⁸ Yes, and you will be brought before governors and kings for my sake, for a testimony to them and to the nations. ¹⁹ But when they deliver you up, don't be anxious how or what you will say, for it will be given you in that hour what you will say. ²⁰ For it is not you who speak, but the Spirit of your Father who speaks in you. ²¹ "Brother will deliver up brother to death, and the father his child. Children will rise up against parents, and cause them to be put to death. ²² You will be hated by all men for my name's sake, but he who endures to the end will be saved. ²³ But when they persecute you in this city, flee into the next, for most certainly I tell you, you will not have gone through the cities of Israel, until the Son of Man has come. ²⁴ "A disciple is not above his teacher, nor a ser-vant above his lord. ²⁵ It is enough for the disciple that he be like his teacher, and the servant like his lord. If they have called the master of the house Beelzebul, how much more those of his household! ²⁶ Therefore don't be afraid of them, for there is nothing covered that will not be revealed; and hidden that will not be known. ²⁷ What I tell you in the darkness, speak in the light; and what you hear whispered in the ear, proclaim on the housetops. ²⁸ Don't be afraid of those who kill the body, but are not able to kill the soul. Rather, fear him who is able to destroy both soul and body in Gehenna. ²⁹ "Aren't two spar-rows sold for an assarion coin? Not one of them falls on the ground apart from your Father's will, ³⁰ but the very hairs of your head are all numbered. ³¹ Therefore don't be afraid. You are of more value than many sparrows. ³² Everyone therefore who confesses me before men, him I will also confess before my Father who is in heaven. ³³ But whoever denies me before men, him I will also deny before my Father who is in heaven. ³⁴ "Don't think that I came to send peace on the earth. I didn't come to send peace, but a sword. ³⁵ For I came to set a man at odds against his father, and a daughter against her mother, and a daughter-in-law against her mother-in-law. ³⁶ A man's foes will be those of his own household. ³⁷ He who loves father or *mother more than me is not worthy of me; and he who loves son or daughter more than me isn't worthy of me. [38] He who doesn't take his cross and follow after me, isn't worthy of me. [39] He who seeks his life will lose it; and he who loses his life for my sake will find it. [40] He who receives you receives me, and he who receives me receives him who sent me. [41] He who receives a prophet in the name of a prophet will receive a prophet's reward. He who receives a righteous man in the name of a righteous man will receive a righteous man's reward. [42] Whoever gives one of these little ones just a cup of cold water to drink in the name of a disciple, most certainly I tell you he will in no way lose his reward."*

John the Baptist Beheaded
- **Mark 6: 14-29 (Matthew 14: 1-12; Luke 9: 7-9)**

[14] King Herod heard this, for his name had become known, and he said, "John the Baptizer has risen from the dead, and therefore these powers are at work in him." [15] But others said, "He is Elijah." Others said, "He is a prophet, or like one of the prophets." [16] But Herod, when he heard this, said, "This is John, whom I beheaded. He has risen from the dead." [17] For Herod himself had sent out and arrested John, and bound him in prison for the sake of Herodias, his brother Philip's wife, for he had married her. [18] For John said to Herod, "It is not lawful for you to have your brother's wife." [19] Herodias set herself against him, and desired to kill him, but she couldn't, [20] for Herod feared John, knowing that he was a righteous and holy man, and kept him safe. When he heard him, he did many things, and he heard him gladly. [21] Then a convenient day came, that Herod on his birthday made a supper for his nobles, the high officers, and the chief men of Galilee. [22] When the daughter of Herodias herself came in and danced, she pleased Herod and those sitting with him. The king said to the young lady, "Ask me whatever you want, and I will give it to you." [23] He swore to her, "Whatever you shall ask of me, I will give you, up to half of my kingdom." [24] She went out, and said to her mother, "What shall I ask?" She said, "The head of John the Baptizer." [25] She came in immediately with haste to the king, and asked, "I want you to give me right now the head of John the Baptizer on a platter." [26] The king was exceedingly sorry, but for the

sake of his oaths, and of his dinner guests, he didn't wish to refuse her. [27] Immediately the king sent out a soldier of his guard, and commanded to bring John's head, and he went and beheaded him in the prison, [28] and brought his head on a platter, and gave it to the young lady; and the young lady gave it to her mother. [29] When his disciples heard this, they came and took up his corpse, and laid it in a tomb.

Jesus Feeds the Five Thousand
- **John 6: 1-15 (Matthew 14: 13-21; Mark 6: 30-44; Luke 9: 10-17)**

[1] After these things, Jesus went away to the other side of the sea of Galilee, which is also called the Sea of Tiberias. [2] A great multitude followed him, because they saw his signs which he did on those who were sick. [3] Jesus went up into the mountain, and he sat there with his disciples. [4] Now the Passover, the feast of the Jews, was at hand. [5] Jesus therefore lifting up his eyes, and seeing that a great multitude was coming to him, said to Philip, *"Where are we to buy bread, that these may eat?"* [6] This he said to test him, for he himself knew what he would do. [7] Philip answered him, "Two hundred denarii worth of bread is not sufficient for them, that everyone of them may receive a little." [8] One of his disciples, Andrew, Simon Peter's brother, said to him, [9] "There is a boy here who has five barley loaves and two fish, but what are these among so many?" [0] Jesus said, *"Have the people sit down."* Now there was much grass in that place. So the men sat down, in number about five thousand. [11] Jesus took the loaves; and having given thanks, he distributed to the disciples, and the disciples to those who were sitting down; likewise also of the fish as much as they desired. [12] When they were filled, he said to his disciples, *"Gather up the broken pieces which are left over, that nothing be lost."* [13] So they gathered them up, and filled twelve baskets with broken pieces from the five barley loaves, which were left over by those who had eaten. [14] When therefore the people saw the sign which Jesus did, they said, "This is truly the prophet who comes into the world." [15] Jesus therefore, perceiving that they were about to come and take him by force, to make him king, withdrew again to the mountain by himself.

Jesus Walks on Water
- **Matthew 14: 22-33 (Mark 6: 45-52; John 6: 16-21)**

[22] Immediately Jesus made the disciples get into the boat, and to go ahead of him to the other side, while he sent the multitudes away. [23] After he had sent the multitudes away, he went up into the mountain by himself to pray. When evening had come, he was there alone. [24] But the boat was now in the middle of the sea, distressed by the waves, for the wind was contrary. [25] In the fourth watch of the night, Jesus came to them, walking on the sea. [26] When the disciples saw him walking on the sea, they were troubled, saying, "It's a ghost!" and they cried out for fear. [27] But immediately Jesus spoke to them, saying *"Cheer up! It is I! Don't be afraid."* [28] Peter answered him and said, "Lord, if it is you, command me to come to you on the waters." [29] He said, *"Come!"* Peter stepped down from the boat, and walked on the waters to come to Jesus. [30] But when he saw that the wind was strong, he was afraid, and beginning to sink, he cried out, saying, "Lord, save me!" [31] Immediately Jesus stretched out his hand, took hold of him, and said to him, *"You of little faith, why did you doubt?"* [32] When they got up into the boat, the wind ceased. [33] Those who were in the boat came and worshiped him, saying, "You are truly the Son of God!"

All who Touched Him
- **Matthew 14: 34-36 (Mark 6: 53-56)**

[34] When they had crossed over, they came to the land of Gennesaret. [35] When the people of that place recognized him, they sent into all that surrounding region, and brought to him all who were sick, [36] and they begged him that they might just touch the fringe of his garment. As many as touched it were made whole.

The Bread of Life
- **John 6: 22-59**

[22] On the next day, the multitude that stood on the other side of the sea saw that there was no other boat there, except the one in which his disciples had embarked, and that Jesus hadn't entered with his disciples into the boat, but his disciples had gone away alone. [23] However boats from Tiberias came near to the place where they ate

the bread after the Lord had given thanks. ²⁴ When the multitude therefore saw that Jesus wasn't there, nor his disciples, they themselves got into the boats, and came to Capernaum, seeking Jesus. ²⁵ When they found him on the other side of the sea, they asked him, "Rabbi, when did you come here?" ²⁶ Jesus answered them, *"Most certainly I tell you, you seek me, not because you saw signs, but because you ate of the loaves, and were filled. ²⁷ Don't work for the food which perishes, but for the food which remains to eternal life, which the Son of Man will give to you. For God the Father has sealed him."* ²⁸ They said therefore to him, "What must we do, that we may work the works of God?" ²⁹ Jesus answered them, *"This is the work of God, that you believe in him whom he has sent."* ³⁰ They said therefore to him, "What then do you do for a sign, that we may see, and believe you? What work do you do? ³¹ Our fathers ate the manna in the wilderness. As it is written, 'He gave them bread out of heaven to eat.'" ³² Jesus therefore said to them, *"Most certainly, I tell you, it wasn't Moses who gave you the bread out of heaven, but my Father gives you the true bread out of heaven. ³³ For the bread of God is that which comes down out of heaven, and gives life to the world."* ³⁴ They said therefore to him, "Lord, always give us this bread." ³⁵ Jesus said to them, *"I am the bread of life. He who comes to me will not be hungry, and he who believes in me will never be thirsty. ³⁶ But I told you that you have seen me, and yet you don't believe. ³⁷ All those whom the Father gives me will come to me. He who comes to me I will in no way throw out. ³⁸ For I have come down from heaven, not to do my own will, but the will of him who sent me. ³⁹ This is the will of my Father who sent me, that of all he has given to me I should lose nothing, but should raise him up at the last day. ⁴⁰ This is the will of the one who sent me, that everyone who sees the Son, and believes in him, should have eternal life; and I will raise him up at the last day."* ⁴¹ The Jews therefore murmured concerning him, because he said, *"I am the bread which came down out of heaven."* ⁴² They said, "Isn't this Jesus, the son of Joseph, whose father and mother we know? How then does he say, 'I have come down out of heaven?'" ⁴³ Therefore Jesus answered them, *"Don't murmur among yourselves. ⁴⁴ No one can come to me unless the Father who sent me draws him, and I will raise him up in the last* day. *45 It is written in the prophets, 'They will all be taught by God.' Therefore everyone who hears from the Father, and has learned, comes to me. 46 Not that anyone has seen the Father, except he who is from God. He has seen the Father. 47 Most certainly, I tell you, he who believes in me has eternal life. 48 I am the bread of life. 49 Your fathers ate the manna in the wilderness, and they died. 50 This is the bread which comes down out of heaven, that anyone may eat of it and not die. 51 I am the living bread which came down out of heaven. If anyone eats of this bread, he will live forever. Yes, the bread which I will give for the life of the world is my flesh."* 52 The Jews therefore contended with one another, saying, "How can this man give us his flesh to eat?" 53 Jesus therefore said to them, *"Most certainly I tell you, unless you eat the flesh of the Son of Man and drink his blood, you don't have life in yourselves. 54 He who eats my flesh and drinks my blood has eternal life, and I will raise him up at the last day. 55 For my flesh is food indeed, and my blood is drink indeed. 56 He who eats my flesh and drinks my blood lives in me, and I in him. 57 As the living Father sent me, and I live because of the Father; so he who feeds on me, he will also live because of me. 58 This is the bread which came down out of heaven—not as our fathers ate the manna, and died. He who eats this bread will live forever."* 59 He said these things in the synagogue, as he taught in Capernaum.

Many Disciples Desert Jesus
  • **John 6: 60-71**

60 Therefore many of his disciples, when they heard this, said, "This is a hard saying! Who can listen to it?" 61 But Jesus knowing in himself that his disciples murmured at this, said to them, *"Does this cause you to stumble? 62 Then what if you would see the Son of Man ascending to where he was before? 63 It is the spirit who gives life. The flesh profits nothing. The words that I speak to you are spirit, and are life. 64 But there are some of you who don't believe."* For Jesus knew from the beginning who they were who didn't believe, and who it was who would betray him. 65 He said, *"For this cause have I said to you that no one can come to me, unless it is given to him by my Father."* 66 At this, many of his disciples went back, and walked no more with him. 67 Jesus said therefore to the twelve, *"You*

don't also want to go away, do you?" ⁶⁸ Simon Peter answered him, "Lord, to whom would we go? You have the words of eternal life. ⁶⁹ We have come to believe and know that you are the Christ, the Son of the living God." ⁷⁰ Jesus answered them, *"Didn't I choose you, the twelve, and one of you is a devil?"* ⁷¹ Now he spoke of Judas, the son of Simon Iscariot, for it was he who would betray him, being one of the twelve.

Jesus' Brothers Disbelieve
- **John 7: 1-9**

¹ After these things, Jesus was walking in Galilee, for he wouldn't walk in Judea, because the Jews sought to kill him. ² Now the feast of the Jews, the Feast of Booths, was at hand. ³ His brothers therefore said to him, "Depart from here, and go into Judea, that your disciples also may see your works which you do. ⁴ For no one does anything in secret, and himself seeks to be known openly. If you do these things, reveal yourself to the world." ⁵ For even his brothers didn't believe in him. ⁶ Jesus therefore said to them, *"My time has not yet come, but your time is always ready. ⁷ The world can't hate you, but it hates me, because I testify about it, that its works are evil. ⁸ You go up to the feast. I am not yet going up to this feast, because my time is not yet fulfilled."* ⁹ Having said these things to them, he stayed in Galilee.

Jesus at the Feast of Tabernacles
- **John 7: 10-24**

¹⁰ But when his brothers had gone up to the feast, then he also went up, not publicly, but as it were in secret. ¹¹ The Jews therefore sought him at the feast, and said, "Where is he?" ¹² There was much murmuring among the multitudes concerning him. Some said, "He is a good man." Others said, "Not so, but he leads the multitude astray." ¹³ Yet no one spoke openly of him for fear of the Jews. ¹⁴ But when it was now the midst of the feast, Jesus went up into the temple and taught. ¹⁵ The Jews therefore marveled, saying, "How does this man know letters, having never been educated?" ¹⁶ Jesus therefore answered them, *"My teaching is not mine, but his who sent me. ¹⁷ If anyone desires to do his will, he will know about the teaching,*

whether it is from God, or if I am speaking from myself. ¹⁸ He who speaks from himself seeks his own glory, but he who seeks the glory of him who sent him is true, and no unrighteousness is in him. ¹⁹ Didn't Moses give you the law, and yet none of you keeps the law? Why do you seek to kill me?" ²⁰ The multitude answered, "You have a demon! Who seeks to kill you?" ²¹ Jesus answered them, *"I did one work, and you all marvel because of it. ²² Moses has given you circumcision (not that it is of Moses, but of the fathers), and on the Sabbath you circumcise a boy. ²³ If a boy receives circumcision on the Sabbath, that the law of Moses may not be broken, are you angry with me, because I made a man completely healthy on the Sabbath? ²⁴ Don't judge according to appearance, but judge righteous judgment."*

Division Over Jesus
• **John 7: 25-44**

²⁵ Therefore some of them of Jerusalem said, "Isn't this he whom they seek to kill? ²⁶ Behold, he speaks openly, and they say nothing to him. Can it be that the rulers indeed know that this is truly the Christ? ²⁷ However we know where this man comes from, but when the Christ comes, no one will know where he comes from." ²⁸ Jesus therefore cried out in the temple, teaching and saying, *"You both know me, and know where I am from. I have not come of myself, but he who sent me is true, whom you don't know. ²⁹ I know him, because I am from him, and he sent me."* ³⁰ They sought therefore to take him; but no one laid a hand on him, because his hour had not yet come. ³¹ But of the multitude, many believed in him. They said, "When the Christ comes, he won't do more signs than those which this man has done, will he?" ³² The Pharisees heard the multitude murmuring these things concerning him, and the chief priests and the Pharisees sent officers to arrest him. ³³ Then Jesus said, *"I will be with you a little while longer, then I go to him who sent me. ³⁴ You will seek me, and won't find me; and where I am, you can't come."* ³⁵ The Jews therefore said among themselves, "Where will this man go that we won't find him? Will he go to the Dispersion among the Greeks, and teach the Greeks? ³⁶ What is this word that he said, *'You will seek me, and won't find me; and where I am, you can't come'?"*

[37] Now on the last and greatest day of the feast, Jesus stood and cried out, *"If anyone is thirsty, let him come to me and drink! [38] He who believes in me, as the Scripture has said, from within him will flow rivers of living water."* [39] But he said this about the Spirit, which those believing in him were to receive. For the Holy Spirit was not yet given, because Jesus wasn't yet glorified. [40] Many of the multitude therefore, when they heard these words, said, "This is truly the prophet." [41] Others said, "This is the Christ." But some said, "What, does the Christ come out of Galilee? [42] Hasn't the Scripture said that the Christ comes of the seed of David, and from Bethlehem, the village where David was?" [43] So there arose a division in the multitude because of him. [44] Some of them would have arrested him, but no one laid hands on him.

Unbelief of the Jewish Leaders
- **John 7: 45-53**

[45] The officers therefore came to the chief priests and Pharisees, and they said to them, "Why didn't you bring him?" [46] The officers answered, "No man ever spoke like this man!" [47] The Pharisees therefore answered them, "You aren't also led astray, are you? [48] Have any of the rulers believed in him, or of the Pharisees? [49] But this multitude that doesn't know the law is accursed." [50] Nicodemus (he who came to him by night, being one of them) said to them, [51] "Does our law judge a man, unless it first hears from him personally and knows what he does?" [52] They answered him, "Are you also from Galilee? Search, and see that no prophet has arisen out of Galilee." [53] Everyone went to his own house,

An Adulterous Woman
- **John 8: 1-11**

[1] but Jesus went to the Mount of Olives. [2] Now very early in the morning, he came again into the temple, and all the people came to him. He sat down, and taught them. [3] The scribes and the Pharisees brought a woman taken in adultery. Having set her in the midst, [4] they told him, "Teacher, we found this woman in adultery, in the very act. [5] Now in our law, Moses commanded us to stone such. What then do you say about her?" [6] They said this testing him, that they

might have something to accuse him of. But Jesus stooped down, and wrote on the ground with his finger. [7] But when they continued asking him, he looked up and said to them, *"He who is without sin among you, let him throw the first stone at her."* [8] Again he stooped down, and with his finger wrote on the ground. [9] They, when they heard it, being convicted by their conscience, went out one by one, beginning from the oldest, even to the last. Jesus was left alone with the woman where she was, in the middle. [10] Jesus, standing up, saw her and said, *"Woman, where are your accusers? Did no one condemn you?"* [11] She said, "No one, Lord." Jesus said, *"Neither do I condemn you. Go your way. From now on, sin no more."*

Light of the World
  • **John 8: 12-20**

[12] Again, therefore, Jesus spoke to them, saying, *"I am the light of the world. He who follows me will not walk in the darkness, but will have the light of life."* [13] The Pharisees therefore said to him, "You testify about yourself. Your testimony is not valid." [14] Jesus answered them, *"Even if I testify about myself, my testimony is true, for I know where I came from, and where I am going; but you don't know where I came from, or where I am going. [15] You judge according to the flesh. I judge no one. [16] Even if I do judge, my judgment is true, for I am not alone, but I am with the Father who sent me. [17] It's also written in your law that the testimony of two people is valid. [18] I am one who testifies about myself, and the Father who sent me testifies about me."* [19] They said therefore to him, "Where is your Father?" Jesus answered, *"You know neither me, nor my Father. If you knew me, you would know my Father also."* [20] Jesus spoke these words in the treasury, as he taught in the temple. Yet no one arrested him, because his hour had not yet come.

Coming Judgment
  • **John 8: 21-30**

[21] Jesus said therefore again to them, *"I am going away, and you will seek me, and you will die in your sins. Where I go, you can't come."* [22] The Jews therefore said, "Will he kill himself, that he says, 'Where I am going, you can't come?'" [23] He said to them, *"You are*

from beneath. I am from above. You are of this world. I am not of this world. ²⁴ *I said therefore to you that you will die in your sins; for unless you believe that I am he, you will die in your sins."* ²⁵ They said therefore to him, "Who are you?" Jesus said to them, *"Just what I have been saying to you from the beginning.* ²⁶ *I have many things to speak and to judge concerning you. However he who sent me is true; and the things which I heard from him, these I say to the world."* ²⁷ They didn't understand that he spoke to them about the Father. ²⁸ Jesus therefore said to them, *"When you have lifted up the Son of Man, then you will know that I am he, and I do nothing of myself, but as my Father taught me, I say these things.* ²⁹ *He who sent me is with me. The Father hasn't left me alone, for I always do the things that are pleasing to him."* ³⁰ As he spoke these things, many believed in him.

Children of Abraham
  • **John 8: 31-41**
³¹ Jesus therefore said to those Jews who had believed him, *"If you remain in my word, then you are truly my disciples.* ³² *You will know the truth, and the truth will make you free."* ³³ They answered him, "We are Abraham's seed, and have never been in bondage to anyone. How do you say, 'You will be made free?'" ³⁴ Jesus answered them, *"Most certainly I tell you, everyone who commits sin is the bond-servant of sin.* ³⁵ *A bondservant doesn't live in the house forever. A son remains forever.* ³⁶ *If therefore the Son makes you free, you will be free indeed.* ³⁷ *I know that you are Abraham's seed, yet you seek to kill me, because my word finds no place in you.* ³⁸ *I say the things which I have seen with my Father; and you also do the things which you have seen with your father."* ³⁹ They answered him, "Our father is Abraham." Jesus said to them, *"If you were Abraham's children, you would do the works of Abraham.* ⁴⁰ *But now you seek to kill me, a man who has told you the truth, which I heard from God. Abraham didn't do this.* ⁴¹ *You do the works of your father."* They said to him, "We were not born of sexual immorality. We have one Father, God."

Children of Satan
- **John 8: 42-47**

[42] Therefore Jesus said to them, *"If God were your father, you would love me, for I came out and have come from God. For I haven't come of myself, but he sent me. [43] Why don't you understand my speech? Because you can't hear my word. [44] You are of your father, the devil, and you want to do the desires of your father. He was a murderer from the beginning, and doesn't stand in the truth, because there is no truth in him. When he speaks a lie, he speaks on his own; for he is a liar, and its father. [45] But because I tell the truth, you don't believe me. [46] Which of you convicts me of sin? If I tell the truth, why do you not believe me? [47] He who is of God hears the words of God. For this cause you don't hear, because you are not of God."*

Jesus' Claims About Himself
- **John 8: 48-59**

[48] Then the Jews answered him, "Don't we say well that you are a Samaritan, and have a demon?" [49] Jesus answered, *"I don't have a demon, but I honor my Father, and you dishonor me. [50] But I don't seek my own glory. There is one who seeks and judges. [51] Most certainly, I tell you, if a person keeps my word, he will never see death."* [52] Then the Jews said to him, "Now we know that you have a demon. Abraham died, and the prophets; and you say, 'If a man keeps my word, he will never taste of death.' [53] Are you greater than our father, Abraham, who died? The prophets died. Who do you make yourself out to be?" [54] Jesus answered, *"If I glorify myself, my glory is nothing. It is my Father who glorifies me, of whom you say that he is our God. [55] You have not known him, but I know him. If I said, 'I don't know him,' I would be like you, a liar. But I know him, and keep his word. [56] Your father Abraham rejoiced to see my day. He saw it, and was glad."* [57] The Jews therefore said to him, "You are not yet fifty years old, and have you seen Abraham?" [58] Jesus said to them, *"Most certainly, I tell you, before Abraham came into existence, I AM."* [59] Therefore they took up stones to throw at him, but Jesus was hidden, and went out of the temple, having gone through their midst, and so passed by.

Jesus Heals a Man Born Blind
- **John 9: 1-12**

¹ As he passed by, he saw a man blind from birth. ² His disciples asked him, "Rabbi, who sinned, this man or his parents, that he was born blind?" ³ Jesus answered, *"Neither did this man sin, nor his parents; but, that the works of God might be revealed in him. ⁴ I must work the works of him who sent me, while it is day. The night is coming, when no one can work. ⁵ While I am in the world, I am the light of the world."* ⁶ When he had said this, he spat on the ground, made mud with the saliva, anointed the blind man's eyes with the mud, ⁷ and said to him, *"Go, wash in the pool of Siloam"* (which means "Sent"). So he went away, washed, and came back seeing. ⁸ The neighbors therefore, and those who saw that he was blind before, said, "Isn't this he who sat and begged?" ⁹ Others were saying, "It is he." Still others were saying, "He looks like him." He said, "I am he." ¹⁰ They therefore were asking him, "How were your eyes opened?" ¹¹ He answered, "A man called Jesus made mud, anointed my eyes, and said to me, *'Go to the pool of Siloam, and wash.'* So I went away and washed, and I received sight." ¹² Then they asked him, "Where is he?" He said, "I don't know."

The Pharisees Investigate the Healing
- **John 9: 13-34**

¹³ They brought him who had been blind to the Pharisees. ¹⁴ It was a Sabbath when Jesus made the mud and opened his eyes. ¹⁵ Again therefore the Pharisees also asked him how he received his sight. He said to them, "He put mud on my eyes, I washed, and I see." ¹⁶ Some therefore of the Pharisees said, "This man is not from God, because he doesn't keep the Sabbath." Others said, "How can a man who is a sinner do such signs?" There was division among them. ⁷ Therefore they asked the blind man again, "What do you say about him, because he opened your eyes?" He said, "He is a prophet." ¹⁸ The Jews therefore did not believe concerning him, that he had been blind, and had received his sight, until they called the parents of him who had received his sight, ¹⁹ and asked them, "Is this your son, whom you say was born blind? How then does he now see?" ²⁰ His parents answered them, "We know that this is our son, and

that he was born blind; [21] but how he now sees, we don't know; or who opened his eyes, we don't know. He is of age. Ask him. He will speak for himself." [22] His parents said these things because they feared the Jews; for the Jews had already agreed that if any man would confess him as Christ, he would be put out of the synagogue. [23] Therefore his parents said, "He is of age. Ask him." [24] So they called the man who was blind a second time, and said to him, "Give glory to God. We know that this man is a sinner." [25] He therefore answered, "I don't know if he is a sinner. One thing I do know: that though I was blind, now I see." [26] They said to him again, "What did he do to you? How did he open your eyes?" [27] He answered them, "I told you already, and you didn't listen. Why do you want to hear it again? You don't also want to become his disciples, do you?" [28] They insulted him and said, "You are his disciple, but we are disciples of Moses. [29] We know that God has spoken to Moses. But as for this man, we don't know where he comes from." [30] The man answered them, "How amazing! You don't know where he comes from, yet he opened my eyes. [31] We know that God doesn't listen to sinners, but if anyone is a worshiper of God, and does his will, he listens to him. [32] Since the world began it has never been heard of that anyone opened the eyes of someone born blind. [33] If this man were not from God, he could do nothing." [34] They answered him, "You were altogether born in sins, and do you teach us?" They threw him out.

Spiritual Blindness
  • **John 9: 35-41**

[35] Jesus heard that they had thrown him out, and finding him, he said, *"Do you believe in the Son of God?"* [36] He answered, "Who is he, Lord, that I may believe in him?" [37] Jesus said to him, *"You have both seen him, and it is he who speaks with you."* [38] He said, "Lord, I believe!" and he worshiped him. [39] Jesus said, *"I came into this world for judgment, that those who don't see may see; and that those who see may become blind."* [40] Those of the Pharisees who were with him heard these things, and said to him, "Are we also blind?" [41] Jesus said to them, *"If you were blind, you would have no sin; but now you say, 'We see.' Therefore your sin remains.*

The Good Shepherd
- **John 10: 1-21**

¹ "Most certainly, I tell you, one who doesn't enter by the door into the sheep fold, but climbs up some other way, the same is a thief and a robber. ² But one who enters in by the door is the shepherd of the sheep. ³ The gatekeeper opens the gate for him, and the sheep listen to his voice. He calls his own sheep by name, and leads them out. ⁴ Whenever he brings out his own sheep, he goes before them, and the sheep follow him, for they know his voice. ⁵ They will by no means follow a stranger, but will flee from him; for they don't know the voice of strangers." ⁶ Jesus spoke this parable to them, but they didn't understand what he was telling them. ⁷ Jesus therefore said to them again, *"Most certainly, I tell you, I am the sheep's door. ⁸ All who came before me are thieves and robbers, but the sheep didn't listen to them. ⁹ I am the door. If anyone enters in by me, he will be saved, and will go in and go out, and will find pasture. ¹⁰ The thief only comes to steal, kill, and destroy. I came that they may have life, and may have it abundantly. ¹¹ I am the good shepherd. The good shepherd lays down his life for the sheep. ¹² He who is a hired hand, and not a shepherd, who doesn't own the sheep, sees the wolf coming, leaves the sheep, and flees. The wolf snatches the sheep, and scatters them. ¹³ The hired hand flees because he is a hired hand, and doesn't care for the sheep. ¹⁴ I am the good shepherd. I know my own, and I'm known by my own; ¹⁵ even as the Father knows me, and I know the Father. I lay down my life for the sheep. ¹⁶ I have other sheep, which are not of this fold. I must bring them also, and they will hear my voice. They will become one flock with one shepherd. ¹⁷ Therefore the Father loves me, because I lay down my life, that I may take it again. ¹⁸ No one takes it away from me, but I lay it down by myself. I have power to lay it down, and I have power to take it again. I received this commandment from my Father."* ¹⁹ Therefore a division arose again among the Jews because of these words. ²⁰ Many of them said, "He has a demon, and is insane! Why do you listen to him?" ²¹ Others said, "These are not the sayings of one possessed by a demon. It isn't possible for a demon to open the eyes of the blind, is it?"

Conflict Over Jesus
- ### John 10: 22-42

²² It was the Feast of the Dedication at Jerusalem. ²³ It was winter, and Jesus was walking in the temple, in Solomon's porch. ²⁴ The Jews therefore came around him and said to him, "How long will you hold us in suspense? If you are the Christ, tell us plainly." ²⁵ Jesus answered them, *"I told you, and you don't believe. The works that I do in my Father's name, these testify about me. ²⁶ But you don't believe, because you are not of my sheep, as I told you. ²⁷ My sheep hear my voice, and I know them, and they follow me. ²⁸ I give eternal life to them. They will never perish, and no one will snatch them out of my hand. ²⁹ My Father, who has given them to me, is greater than all. No one is able to snatch them out of my Father's hand. ³⁰ I and the Father are one."* ³¹ Therefore Jews took up stones again to stone him. ³² Jesus answered them, *"I have shown you many good works from my Father. For which of those works do you stone me?"* ³³ The Jews answered him, "We don't stone you for a good work, but for blasphemy: because you, being a man, make yourself God." ³⁴ Jesus answered them, *"Isn't it written in your law, 'I said, you are gods?' ³⁵ If he called them gods, to whom the word of God came (and the Scripture can't be broken), ³⁶ do you say of him whom the Father sanctified and sent into the world, 'You blaspheme,' because I said, 'I am the Son of God?' ³⁷ If I don't do the works of my Father, don't believe me. ³⁸ But if I do them, though you don't believe me, believe the works; that you may know and believe that the Father is in me, and I in the Father."* ³⁹ They sought again to seize him, and he went out of their hand. ⁴⁰ He went away again beyond the Jordan into the place where John was baptizing at first, and there he stayed. ⁴¹ Many came to him. They said, "John indeed did no sign, but everything that John said about this man is true." ⁴² Many believed in him there.

Clean and Unclean
- ### Mark 7: 1-23 (Matthew 15: 1-20)

¹ Then the Pharisees, and some of the scribes gathered together to him, having come from Jerusalem. ² Now when they saw some of his disciples eating bread with defiled, that is, unwashed, hands, they found fault. ³ (For the Pharisees, and all the Jews, don't eat unless

they wash their hands and forearms, holding to the tradition of the elders. [4]They don't eat when they come from the marketplace, unless they bathe themselves, and there are many other things, which they have received to hold to: washings of cups, pitchers, bronze vessels, and couches.) [5]The Pharisees and the scribes asked him, "Why don't your disciples walk according to the tradition of the elders, but eat their bread with unwashed hands?" [6]He answered them, *"Well did Isaiah prophesy of you hypocrites, as it is written, 'This people honors me with their lips, but their heart is far from me. [7] But in vain do they worship me, teaching as doctrines the commandments of men.'* [8] *"For you set aside the commandment of God, and hold tightly to the tradition of men—the washing of pitchers and cups, and you do many other such things."* [9]He said to them, *"Full well do you reject the commandment of God, that you may keep your tradition. [10]For Moses said, 'Honor your father and your mother;' and, 'He who speaks evil of father or mother, let him be put to death.' [11] But you say, 'If a man tells his father or his mother, "Whatever profit you might have received from me is Corban, that is to say, given to God";' [12]then you no longer allow him to do anything for his father or his mother, [13] making void the word of God by your tradition, which you have handed down. You do many things like this."* [14]He called all the multitude to himself, and said to them, *"Hear me, all of you, and understand. [15]There is nothing from outside of the man, that going into him can defile him; but the things which proceed out of the man are those that defile the* man. [16] *If anyone has ears to hear, let him hear!"* [17]When he had entered into a house away from the multitude, his disciples asked him about the parable. [18]He said to them, *"Are you thus without understanding also? Don't you perceive that whatever goes into the man from outside can't defile him, [19]because it doesn't go into his heart, but into his stomach, then into the latrine, thus purifying all foods?"* [20]He said, *"That which proceeds out of the man, that defiles the man. [21]For from within, out of the hearts of men, proceed evil thoughts, adulteries, sexual sins, murders, thefts, [22]covetings, wickedness, deceit, lustful desires, an evil eye, blasphemy, pride, and foolishness. [23]All these evil things come from within, and defile the man."*

Faith of a Canaanite Woman
- **Matthew 15: 21-28 (Mark 7: 24-30)**

[21] Jesus went out from there, and withdrew into the region of Tyre and Sidon. [22] Behold, a Canaanite woman came out from those borders, and cried, saying, "Have mercy on me, Lord, you son of David! My daughter is severely demonized!" [23] But he answered her not a word. His disciples came and begged him, saying, "Send her away; for she cries after us." [24] But he answered, *"I wasn't sent to anyone but the lost sheep of the house of Israel."* [25] But she came and worshiped him, saying, "Lord, help me." [26] But he answered, *"It is not appropriate to take the children's bread and throw it to the dogs."* [27] But she said, "Yes, Lord, but even the dogs eat the crumbs which fall from their masters' table." [28] Then Jesus answered her, *"Woman, great is your faith! Be it done to you even as you desire."* And her daughter was healed from that hour.

Jesus Heals a Deaf and Mute Man
- **Mark 7: 31-37 (Matthew 15: 29-31)**

[31] Again he departed from the borders of Tyre and Sidon, and came to the sea of Galilee, through the midst of the region of Decapolis. [32] They brought to him one who was deaf and had an impediment in his speech. They begged him to lay his hand on him. [33] He took him aside from the multitude, privately, and put his fingers into his ears, and he spat, and touched his tongue. [34] Looking up to heaven, he sighed, and said to him, *"Ephphatha!"* that is, *"Be opened!"* [35] Immediately his ears were opened, and the impediment of his tongue was released, and he spoke clearly. [36] He commanded them that they should tell no one, but the more he commanded them, so much the more widely they proclaimed it. [37] They were astonished beyond measure, saying, "He has done all things well. He makes even the deaf hear, and the mute speak!"

Jesus Feeds the Four Thousand
- **Matthew 15: 32-39 (Mark 8: 1-10)**

[32] Jesus summoned his disciples and said, *"I have compassion on the multitude, because they continue with me now three days and have nothing to eat. I don't want to send them away fasting, or they*

might faint on the way." ³³ The disciples said to him, "Where should we get so many loaves in a deserted place as to satisfy so great a multitude?" ³⁴ Jesus said to them, *"How many loaves do you have?"* They said, "Seven, and a few small fish." ³⁵ He commanded the multitude to sit down on the ground; ³⁶ and he took the seven loaves and the fish. He gave thanks and broke them, and gave to the disciples, and the disciples to the multitudes. ³⁷ They all ate, and were filled. They took up seven baskets full of the broken pieces that were left over. ³⁸ Those who ate were four thousand men, besides women and children. ³⁹ Then he sent away the multitudes, got into the boat, and came into the borders of Magdala.

Demand for a Sign
- **Matthew 16: 1-4 (Mark 8: 11-13)**

¹ The Pharisees and Sadducees came, and testing him, asked him to show them a sign from heaven. ² But he answered them, *"When it is evening, you say, 'It will be fair weather, for the sky is red.' ³ In the morning, 'It will be foul weather today, for the sky is red and threatening.' Hypocrites! You know how to discern the appearance of the sky, but you can't discern the signs of the times! ⁴ An evil and adulterous generation seeks after a sign, and there will be no sign given to it, except the sign of the prophet Jonah."* He left them, and departed.

Beware of Some Teachings
- **Matthew 16: 5-12 (Mark 8: 14-21)**

⁵ The disciples came to the other side and had forgotten to take bread. ⁶ Jesus said to them, *"Take heed and beware of the yeast of the Pharisees and Sadducees."* ⁷ They reasoned among themselves, saying, "We brought no bread." ⁸ Jesus, perceiving it, said, *"Why do you reason among yourselves, you of little faith, 'because you have brought no bread?' ⁹ Don't you yet perceive, neither remember the five loaves for the five thousand, and how many baskets you took up? ¹⁰ Nor the seven loaves for the four thousand, and how many baskets you took up? ¹¹ How is it that you don't perceive that I didn't speak to you concerning bread? But beware of the yeast of the Pharisees and Sadducees."* ¹² Then they understood that he didn't tell them to

beware of the yeast of bread, but of the teaching of the Pharisees and Sadducees.

Jesus Heals a Blind Man
  • **Mark 8: 22-26**

²² He came to Bethsaida. They brought a blind man to him, and begged him to touch him. ²³ He took hold of the blind man by the hand, and brought him out of the village. When he had spit on his eyes, and laid his hands on him, he asked him if he saw anything. ²⁴ He looked up, and said, "I see men; for I see them like trees walking." ²⁵ Then again he laid his hands on his eyes. He looked intently, and was restored, and saw everyone clearly. ²⁶ He sent him away to his house, saying, *"Don't enter into the village, nor tell anyone in the village."*

Peter Declares That Jesus is the Messiah
  • **Matthew 16: 13-20 (Mark 8: 27-30; Luke 9: 18-20)**

¹³ Now when Jesus came into the parts of Caesarea Philippi, he asked his disciples, saying, *"Who do men say that I, the Son of Man, am?"* ¹⁴ They said, "Some say John the Baptizer, some, Elijah, and others, Jeremiah, or one of the prophets." ¹⁵ He said to them, *"But who do you say that I am?"* ¹⁶ Simon Peter answered, "You are the Christ, the Son of the living God." ¹⁷ Jesus answered him, *"Blessed are you, Simon Bar Jonah, for flesh and blood has not revealed this to you, but my Father who is in heaven. ¹⁸ I also tell you that you are Peter, and on this rock I will build my assembly, and the gates of Hades will not prevail against it. ¹⁹ I will give to you the keys of the Kingdom of Heaven, and whatever you bind on earth will have been bound in heaven; and whatever you release on earth will have been released in heaven."* ²⁰ Then he commanded the disciples that they should tell no one that he was Jesus the Christ.

Jesus Predicts His Own Death
  • **Matthew 16: 21-28 (Mark 8: 31-38 & 9: 1; Luke 9: 21-27)**

²¹ From that time, Jesus began to show his disciples that he must go to Jerusalem and suffer many things from the elders, chief priests, and scribes, and be killed, and the third day be raised up. ²² Peter

took him aside, and began to rebuke him, saying, "Far be it from you, Lord! This will never be done to you." [23] But he turned, and said to Peter, *"Get behind me, Satan! You are a stumbling block to me, for you are not setting your mind on the things of God, but on the things of men."* [24] Then Jesus said to his disciples, *"If anyone desires to come after me, let him deny himself, and take up his cross, and follow me.* [25] *For whoever desires to save his life will lose it, and whoever will lose his life for my sake will find it.* [26] *For what will it profit a man, if he gains the whole world, and forfeits his life? Or what will a man give in exchange for his life?* [27] *For the Son of Man will come in the glory of his Father with his angels, and then he will render to everyone according to his deeds.* [28] *Most certainly I tell you, there are some standing here who will in no way taste of death, until they see the Son of Man coming in his Kingdom."*

The Transfiguration
  • **Matthew 17: 1-13 (Mark 9: 2-13; Luke 9: 28-36)**
[1] After six days, Jesus took with him Peter, James, and John his brother, and brought them up into a high mountain by themselves. [2] He was transfigured before them. His face shone like the sun, and his garments became as white as the light. [3] Behold, Moses and Elijah appeared to them talking with him. [4] Peter answered, and said to Jesus, "Lord, it is good for us to be here. If you want, let's make three tents here: one for you, one for Moses, and one for Elijah." [5] While he was still speaking, behold, a bright cloud overshadowed them. Behold, a voice came out of the cloud, saying, "This is my beloved Son, in whom I am well pleased. Listen to him." [6] When the disciples heard it, they fell on their faces, and were very afraid. [7] Jesus came and touched them and said, *"Get up, and don't be afraid."* [8] Lifting up their eyes, they saw no one, except Jesus alone. [9] As they were coming down from the mountain, Jesus commanded them, saying, *"Don't tell anyone what you saw, until the Son of Man has risen from the dead."* [10] His disciples asked him, saying, "Then why do the scribes say that Elijah must come first?" [11] Jesus answered them, *"Elijah indeed comes first, and will restore all things,* [12] *but I tell you that Elijah has come already, and they didn't recognize him, but did to him whatever they wanted to. Even so the Son of Man will*

also suffer by them." [13] Then the disciples understood that he spoke to them of John the Baptizer.

Jesus Heals a Boy With an Evil Spirit
- **Mark 9: 14-29 (Matthew 17: 14-21; Luke 9: 37-43a)**

[14] Coming to the disciples, he saw a great multitude around them, and scribes questioning them. [15] Immediately all the multitude, when they saw him, were greatly amazed, and running to him greeted him. [16] He asked the scribes, *"What are you asking them?"* [17] One of the multitude answered, "Teacher, I brought to you my son, who has a mute spirit; [18] and wherever it seizes him, it throws him down, and he foams at the mouth, and grinds his teeth, and wastes away. I asked your disciples to cast it out, and they weren't able." [19] He answered him, *"Unbelieving generation, how long shall I be with you? How long shall I bear with you? Bring him to me."* [20] They brought him to him, and when he saw him, immediately the spirit convulsed him, and he fell on the ground, wallowing and foaming at the mouth. [21] He asked his father, *"How long has it been since this has come to him?"* He said, "From childhood. [22] Often it has cast him both into the fire and into the water, to destroy him. But if you can do anything, have compassion on us, and help us." [23] Jesus said to him, *"If you can believe, all things are possible to him who believes."* [24] Immediately the father of the child cried out with tears, "I believe. Help my unbelief!" [25] When Jesus saw that a multitude came running together, he rebuked the unclean spirit, saying to him, *"You mute and deaf spirit, I command you, come out of him, and never enter him again!"* [26] Having cried out, and convulsed greatly, it came out of him. The boy became like one dead; so much that most of them said, "He is dead." [27] But Jesus took him by the hand, and raised him up; and he arose. [28] When he had come into the house, his disciples asked him privately, "Why couldn't we cast it out?" [29] He said to them, *"This kind can come out by nothing, except by prayer and fasting."*

Jesus Predicts His Death a Second Time
- **Matthew 17: 22-23 (Mark 9: 30-32; Luke 9: 43b-45)**

[22] While they were staying in Galilee, Jesus said to them, *"The Son of Man is about to be delivered up into the hands of men, [23] and they*

will kill him, and the third day he will be raised up." They were exceedingly sorry.

The Temple Tax
- **Matthew 17: 24-27**

[24] When they had come to Capernaum, those who collected the didrachma coins came to Peter, and said, "Doesn't your teacher pay the didrachma?" [25] He said, "Yes." When he came into the house, Jesus anticipated him, saying, *"What do you think, Simon? From whom do the kings of the earth receive toll or tribute? From their children, or from strangers?"* [26] Peter said to him, "From strangers." Jesus said to him, *"Therefore the children are exempt.* [27] *But, lest we cause them to stumble, go to the sea, cast a hook, and take up the first fish that comes up. When you have opened its mouth, you will find a stater coin. Take that, and give it to them for me and you."*

Greatest in the Kingdom of Heaven
- **Mark 9: 33-37 (Matthew 18: 1-5; Luke 9: 46-48)**

[33] He came to Capernaum, and when he was in the house he asked them, *"What were you arguing among yourselves on the way?"* [34] But they were silent, for they had disputed one with another on the way about who was the greatest. [35] He sat down, and called the twelve; and he said to them, *"If any man wants to be first, he shall be last of all, and servant of all."* [36] He took a little child, and set him in their midst. Taking him in his arms, he said to them, [37] *"Whoever receives one such little child in my name, receives me, and whoever receives me, doesn't receive me, but him who sent me."*

Using the Name of Jesus
- **Mark 9: 38-41 (Luke 9: 49-50)**

[38] John said to him, "Teacher, we saw someone who doesn't follow us casting out demons in your name; and we forbade him, because he doesn't follow us." [39] But Jesus said, *"Don't forbid him, for there is no one who will do a mighty work in my name, and be able quickly to speak evil of me.* [40] *For whoever is not against us is on our side.* [41] *For whoever will give you a cup of water to drink in my name,*

because you are Christ's, most certainly I tell you, he will in no way lose his reward.

Warnings Against Temptation
- ## Mark 9: 42-50 (Matthew 18: 6-11; Luke 17: 1-2)

[42] Whoever will cause one of these little ones who believe in me to stumble, it would be better for him if he were thrown into the sea with a millstone hung around his neck. [43] If your hand causes you to stumble, cut it off. It is better for you to enter into life maimed, rather than having your two hands to go into Gehenna, into the unquenchable fire, [44] 'where their worm doesn't die, and the fire is not quenched.' [45] If your foot causes you to stumble, cut it off. It is better for you to enter into life lame, rather than having your two feet to be cast into Gehenna, into the fire that will never be quenched— [46] 'where their worm doesn't die, and the fire is not quenched.' [47] If your eye causes you to stumble, cast it out. It is better for you to enter into the Kingdom of God with one eye, rather than having two eyes to be cast into the Gehenna of fire, [48] 'where their worm doesn't die, and the fire is not quenched.' [49] For everyone will be salted with fire, and every sacrifice will be seasoned with salt. [50] Salt is good, but if the salt has lost its saltiness, with what will you season it? Have salt in yourselves, and be at peace with one another."

Dealing With Sin in the Church
- ## Matthew 18: 15-20

[15] "If your brother sins against you, go, show him his fault between you and him alone. If he listens to you, you have gained back your brother. [16] But if he doesn't listen, take one or two more with you, that at the mouth of two or three witnesses every word may be established. [17] If he refuses to listen to them, tell it to the assembly. If he refuses to hear the assembly also, let him be to you as a Gentile or a tax collector. [18] Most certainly I tell you, whatever things you bind on earth will have been bound in heaven, and whatever things you release on earth will have been released in heaven. [19] Again, assuredly I tell you, that if two of you will agree on earth concerning anything that they will ask, it will be done for them by my Father who

is in heaven. *²⁰ For where two or three are gathered together in my name, there I am in their midst."*

The Unmerciful Servant
- **Matthew 18: 21-35 (Luke 17: 3-4)**

²¹ Then Peter came and said to him, "Lord, how often shall my brother sin against me, and I forgive him? Until seven times?" ²² Jesus said to him, *"I don't tell you until seven times, but, until seventy times seven. ²³ Therefore the Kingdom of Heaven is like a certain king, who wanted to reconcile accounts with his servants. ²⁴ When he had begun to reconcile, one was brought to him who owed him ten thousand talents. ²⁵ But because he couldn't pay, his lord commanded him to be sold, with his wife, his children, and all that he had, and payment to be made. ²⁶ The servant therefore fell down and kneeled before him, saying, 'Lord, have patience with me, and I will repay you all!' ²⁷ The lord of that servant, being moved with compassion, released him, and forgave him the debt. ²⁸ "But that servant went out, and found one of his fellow servants, who owed him one hundred denarii, and he grabbed him, and took him by the throat, saying, 'Pay me what you owe!' ²⁹ "So his fellow servant fell down at his feet and begged him, saying, 'Have patience with me, and I will repay you!' ³⁰ He would not, but went and cast him into prison, until he should pay back that which was due. ³¹ So when his fellow servants saw what was done, they were exceedingly sorry, and came and told to their lord all that was done. ³² Then his lord called him in, and said to him, 'You wicked servant! I forgave you all that debt, because you begged me. ³³ Shouldn't you also have had mercy on your fellow servant, even as I had mercy on you?' ³⁴ His lord was angry, and delivered him to the tormentors, until he should pay all that was due to him. ³⁵ So my heavenly Father will also do to you, if you don't each forgive your brother from your hearts for his misdeeds."*

Samaritan Opposition
- **Luke 9: 51-56**

⁵¹ It came to pass, when the days were near that he should be taken up, he intently set his face to go to Jerusalem, ⁵² and sent messen-

gers before his face. They went, and entered into a village of the Samaritans, so as to prepare for him. [53] They didn't receive him, because he was traveling with his face set towards Jerusalem. [54] When his disciples, James and John, saw this, they said, "Lord, do you want us to command fire to come down from the sky, and destroy them, just as Elijah did?" [55] But he turned and rebuked them, *"You don't know of what kind of spirit you are. [56] For the Son of Man didn't come to destroy men's lives, but to save them."* They went to another village.

The Cost of Following Jesus
 • **Luke 9: 57-62 (Matthew 8: 18-22)**
[57] As they went on the way, a certain man said to him, "I want to follow you wherever you go, Lord." [58] Jesus said to him, *"The foxes have holes, and the birds of the sky have nests, but the Son of Man has no place to lay his head."* [59] He said to another, *"Follow me!"* But he said, "Lord, allow me first to go and bury my father." [60] But Jesus said to him, *"Leave the dead to bury their own dead, but you go and announce the Kingdom of God."* [61] Another also said, "I want to follow you, Lord, but first allow me to say good-bye to those who are at my house." [62] But Jesus said to him, *"No one, having put his hand to the plow, and looking back, is fit for the Kingdom of God."*

Jesus Sends out Seventy Others
 • **Luke 10: 1-24**
[1] Now after these things, the Lord also appointed seventy others, and sent them two by two ahead of him into every city and place, where he was about to come. [2] Then he said to them, *"The harvest is indeed plentiful, but the laborers are few. Pray therefore to the Lord of the harvest, that he may send out laborers into his harvest. [3] Go your ways. Behold, I send you out as lambs among wolves. [4] Carry no purse, nor wallet, nor sandals. Greet no one on the way. [5] Into whatever house you enter, first say, 'Peace be to this house.' [6] If a son of peace is there, your peace will rest on him; but if not, it will return to you. [7] Remain in that same house, eating and drinking the things they give, for the laborer is worthy of his wages. Don't go from house to house. [8] Into whatever city you enter, and they receive you, eat the*

things that are set before you. [9] Heal the sick who are therein, and tell them, 'The Kingdom of God has come near to you.' [10] But into whatever city you enter, and they don't receive you, go out into its streets and say, [11] 'Even the dust from your city that clings to us, we wipe off against you. Nevertheless know this, that the Kingdom of God has come near to you.' [12] I tell you, it will be more tolerable in that day for Sodom than for that city. [13] "Woe to you, Chorazin! Woe to you, Bethsaida! For if the mighty works had been done in Tyre and Sidon which were done in you, they would have repented long ago, sitting in sackcloth and ashes. [14] But it will be more tolerable for Tyre and Sidon in the judgment than for you. [15] You, Capernaum, who are exalted to heaven, will be brought down to Hades. [16] Whoever listens to you listens to me, and whoever rejects you rejects me. Whoever rejects me rejects him who sent me." [17] The seventy returned with joy, saying, "Lord, even the demons are subject to us in your name!" [18] He said to them, *"I saw Satan having fallen like lightning from heaven. [19] Behold, I give you authority to tread on serpents and scorpions, and over all the power of the enemy. Nothing will in any way hurt you. [20] Nevertheless, don't rejoice in this, that the spirits are subject to you, but rejoice that your names are written in heaven."* [21] In that same hour Jesus rejoiced in the Holy Spirit, and said, *"I thank you, O Father, Lord of heaven and earth, that you have hidden these things from the wise and understanding, and revealed them to little children. Yes, Father, for so it was well-pleasing in your sight."* [22] Turning to the disciples, he said, *"All things have been delivered to me by my Father. No one knows who the Son is, except the Father, and who the Father is, except the Son, and he to whomever the Son desires to reveal him."* [23] Turning to the disciples, he said privately, *"Blessed are the eyes which see the things that you see, [24] for I tell you that many prophets and kings desired to see the things which you see, and didn't see them, and to hear the things which you hear, and didn't hear them."*

The Good Samaritan
• Luke 10: 25-37

[25] Behold, a certain lawyer stood up and tested him, saying, "Teacher, what shall I do to inherit eternal life?" [26] He said to him, *"What*

is written in the law? How do you read it?" [27] He answered, "You shall love the Lord your God with all your heart, with all your soul, with all your strength, and with all your mind; and your neighbor as yourself." [28] He said to him, *"You have answered correctly. Do this, and you will live."* [29] But he, desiring to justify himself, asked Jesus, "Who is my neighbor?" [30] Jesus answered, *"A certain man was going down from Jerusalem to Jericho, and he fell among robbers, who both stripped him and beat him, and departed, leaving him half dead. [31] By chance a certain priest was going down that way. When he saw him, he passed by on the other side. [32] In the same way a Levite also, when he came to the place, and saw him, passed by on the other side. [33] But a certain Samaritan, as he traveled, came where he was. When he saw him, he was moved with compassion, [34] came to him, and bound up his wounds, pouring on oil and wine. He set him on his own animal, and brought him to an inn, and took care of him. [35] On the next day, when he departed, he took out two denarii, and gave them to the host, and said to him, 'Take care of him. Whatever you spend beyond that, I will repay you when I return.' [36] Now which of these three do you think seemed to be a neighbor to him who fell among the robbers?"* [37] He said, "He who showed mercy on him." Then Jesus said to him, *"Go and do likewise."*

At the Home of Martha and Mary
• Luke 10: 38-42

[38] It happened as they went on their way, he entered into a certain village, and a certain woman named Martha received him into her house. [39] She had a sister called Mary, who also sat at Jesus' feet, and heard his word. [40] But Martha was distracted with much serving, and she came up to him, and said, "Lord, don't you care that my sister left me to serve alone? Ask her therefore to help me." [41] Jesus answered her, *"Martha, Martha, you are anxious and troubled about many things, [42] but one thing is needed. Mary has chosen the good part, which will not be taken away from her."*

How to Pray
  • **Luke 11: 1-8 (Matthew 6: 5-15)**

[1] It happened, that when he finished praying in a certain place, one of his disciples said to him, "Lord, teach us to pray, just as John also taught his disciples." [2] He said to them, *"When you pray, say, 'Our Father in heaven, may your name be kept holy. May your Kingdom come. May your will be done on earth, as it is in heaven. [3] Give us day by day our daily bread. [4] Forgive us our sins, for we ourselves also forgive everyone who is indebted to us. Bring us not into temptation, but deliver us from the evil one.'"* [5] He said to them, *"Which of you, if you go to a friend at midnight, and tell him, 'Friend, lend me three loaves of bread, [6] for a friend of mine has come to me from a journey, and I have nothing to set before him,' [7] and he from within will answer and say, 'Don't bother me. The door is now shut, and my children are with me in bed. I can't get up and give it to you'? [8] I tell you, although he will not rise and give it to him because he is his friend, yet because of his persistence, he will get up and give him as many as he needs.*

Ask, Seek, and Knock
  • **Luke 11: 9-13 (Matthew 7: 7-11)**

[9] *"I tell you, keep asking, and it will be given you. Keep seeking, and you will find. Keep knocking, and it will be opened to you. [10] For everyone who asks receives. He who seeks finds. To him who knocks it will be opened. [11] "Which of you fathers, if your son asks for bread, will give him a stone? Or if he asks for a fish, he won't give him a snake instead of a fish, will he? [12] Or if he asks for an egg, he won't give him a scorpion, will he? [13] If you then, being evil, know how to give good gifts to your children, how much more will your heavenly Father give the Holy Spirit to those who ask him?"*

Source of Power
  • **Matthew 12: 22-37 (Mark 3: 20-30; Luke 11: 14-23)**

[22] Then one possessed by a demon, blind and mute, was brought to him and he healed him, so that the blind and mute man both spoke and saw. [23] All the multitudes were amazed, and said, "Can this be the son of David?" [24] But when the Pharisees heard it, they said, "This

man does not cast out demons, except by Beelzebul, the prince of the demons." [25] Knowing their thoughts, Jesus said to them, *"Every kingdom divided against itself is brought to desolation, and every city or house divided against itself will not stand. [26] If Satan casts out Satan, he is divided against himself. How then will his kingdom stand? [27] If I by Beelzebul cast out demons, by whom do your children cast them out? Therefore they will be your judges. [28] But if I by the Spirit of God cast out demons, then the Kingdom of God has come upon you. [29] Or how can one enter into the house of the strong man, and plunder his goods, unless he first bind the strong man? Then he will plunder his house. [30] "He who is not with me is against me, and he who doesn't gather with me, scatters. [31] Therefore I tell you, every sin and blasphemy will be forgiven men, but the blasphemy against the Spirit will not be forgiven men. [32] Whoever speaks a word against the Son of Man, it will be forgiven him; but whoever speaks against the Holy Spirit, it will not be forgiven him, neither in this age, nor in that which is to come. [33] "Either make the tree good, and its fruit good, or make the tree corrupt, and its fruit corrupt; for the tree is known by its fruit. [34] You offspring of vipers, how can you, being evil, speak good things? For out of the abundance of the heart, the mouth speaks. [35] The good man out of his good treasure brings out good things, and the evil man out of his evil treasure brings out evil things. [36] I tell you that every idle word that men speak, they will give account of it in the day of judgment. [37] For by your words you will be justified, and by your words you will be condemned."*

A Miraculous Sign
   • **Luke 11: 24-32 (Matthew 12: 38-45)**

[24] *The unclean spirit, when he has gone out of the man, passes through dry places, seeking rest, and finding none, he says, 'I will turn back to my house from which I came out.' [25] When he returns, he finds it swept and put in order. [26] Then he goes, and takes seven other spirits more evil than himself, and they enter in and dwell there. The last state of that man becomes worse than the first."* [27] It came to pass, as he said these things, a certain woman out of the multitude lifted up her voice, and said to him, "Blessed is the womb that bore you, and the breasts which nursed you!" [28] But he said, *"On*

the contrary, blessed are those who hear the word of God, and keep it." [29] When the multitudes were gathering together to him, he began to say, *"This is an evil generation. It seeks after a sign. No sign will be given to it but the sign of Jonah, the prophet. [30] For even as Jonah became a sign to the Ninevites, so will also the Son of Man be to this generation. [31] The Queen of the South will rise up in the judgment with the men of this generation, and will condemn them: for she came from the ends of the earth to hear the wisdom of Solomon; and behold, one greater than Solomon is here. [32] The men of Nineveh will stand up in the judgment with this generation, and will condemn it: for they repented at the preaching of Jonah, and behold, one greater than Jonah is here.*

Lamp of the Body
- ## Luke 11: 33-36

[33] *"No one, when he has lit a lamp, puts it in a cellar or under a basket, but on a stand, that those who come in may see the light. [34] The lamp of the body is the eye. Therefore when your eye is good, your whole body is also full of light; but when it is evil, your body also is full of darkness. [35] Therefore see whether the light that is in you isn't darkness. [36] If therefore your whole body is full of light, having no part dark, it will be wholly full of light, as when the lamp with its bright shining gives you light."*

The Religious Leaders are Criticized
- ## Luke 11: 37-54

[37] Now as he spoke, a certain Pharisee asked him to dine with him. He went in, and sat at the table. [38] When the Pharisee saw it, he marveled that he had not first washed himself before dinner. [39] The Lord said to him, *"Now you Pharisees cleanse the outside of the cup and of the platter, but your inward part is full of extortion and wickedness. [40] You foolish ones, didn't he who made the outside make the inside also? [41] But give for gifts to the needy those things which are within, and behold, all things will be clean to you. [42] But woe to you Pharisees! For you tithe mint and rue and every herb, but you bypass justice and the love of God. You ought to have done these, and not to have left the other undone. [43] Woe to you Pharisees! For*

you love the best seats in the synagogues, and the greetings in the marketplaces. ⁴⁴ *Woe to you, scribes and Pharisees, hypocrites! For you are like hidden graves, and the men who walk over them don't know it."* ⁴⁵ One of the lawyers answered him, "Teacher, in saying this you insult us also." ⁴⁶ He said, *"Woe to you lawyers also! For you load men with burdens that are difficult to carry, and you yourselves won't even lift one finger to help carry those burdens.* ⁴⁷ *Woe to you! For you build the tombs of the prophets, and your fathers killed them.* ⁴⁸ *So you testify and consent to the works of your fathers. For they killed them, and you build their tombs.* ⁴⁹ *Therefore also the wisdom of God said, 'I will send to them prophets and apostles; and some of them they will kill and persecute,* ⁵⁰ *that the blood of all the prophets, which was shed from the foundation of the world, may be required of this generation;* ⁵¹ *from the blood of Abel to the blood of Zachariah, who perished between the altar and the sanctuary.' Yes, I tell you, it will be required of this generation.* ⁵² *Woe to you lawyers! For you took away the key of knowledge. You didn't enter in yourselves, and those who were entering in, you hindered."* ⁵³ As he said these things to them, the scribes and the Pharisees began to be terribly angry, and to draw many things out of him; ⁵⁴ lying in wait for him, and seeking to catch him in something he might say, that they might accuse him.

Warnings and Encouragements
• Luke 12: 1-12

¹ Meanwhile, when a multitude of many thousands had gathered together, so much so that they trampled on each other, he began to tell his disciples first of all, *"Beware of the yeast of the Pharisees, which is hypocrisy.* ² *But there is nothing covered up, that will not be revealed, nor hidden, that will not be known.* ³ *Therefore whatever you have said in the darkness will be heard in the light. What you have spoken in the ear in the inner rooms will be proclaimed on the housetops.* ⁴ *"I tell you, my friends, don't be afraid of those who kill the body, and after that have no more that they can do.* ⁵ *But I will warn you whom you should fear. Fear him, who after he has killed, has power to cast into Gehenna. Yes, I tell you, fear him.* ⁶ *"Aren't five sparrows sold for two assaria coins? Not one of them is forgotten by God.* ⁷ *But the very hairs of your head are all num-*

bered. *Therefore don't be afraid. You are of more value than many sparrows.* [8] *"I tell you, everyone who confesses me before men, him will the Son of Man also confess before the angels of God;* [9] *but he who denies me in the presence of men will be denied in the presence of the angels of God.* [10] *Everyone who speaks a word against the Son of Man will be forgiven, but those who blaspheme against the Holy Spirit will not be forgiven.* [11] *When they bring you before the synagogues, the rulers, and the authorities, don't be anxious how or what you will answer, or what you will say;* [12] *for the Holy Spirit will teach you in that same hour what you must say."*

The Rich Fool
   • **Luke 12: 13-21**
[13] One of the multitude said to him, "Teacher, tell my brother to divide the inheritance with me." [14] But he said to him, *"Man, who made me a judge or an arbitrator over you?"* [15] He said to them, *"Beware! Keep yourselves from covetousness, for a man's life doesn't consist of the abundance of the things which he possesses."* [16] He spoke a parable to them, saying, *"The ground of a certain rich man brought forth abundantly.* [17] *He reasoned within himself, saying, 'What will I do, because I don't have room to store my crops?'* [18] *He said, 'This is what I will do. I will pull down my barns, and build bigger ones, and there I will store all my grain and my goods.* [19] *I will tell my soul, "Soul, you have many goods laid up for many years. Take your ease, eat, drink, be merry."'* [20] *"But God said to him, 'You foolish one, tonight your soul is required of you. The things which you have prepared—whose will they be?'* [21] *So is he who lays up treasure for himself, and is not rich toward God."*

Watchfulness
   • **Luke 12: 35-48**
[35] *"Let your waist be dressed and your lamps burning.* [36] *Be like men watching for their lord, when he returns from the marriage feast; that, when he comes and knocks, they may immediately open to him.* [37] *Blessed are those servants, whom the lord will find watching when he comes. Most certainly I tell you, that he will dress himself, and make them recline, and will come and serve them.* [38] *They will be*

blessed if he comes in the second or third watch, and finds them so. *³⁹ But know this, that if the master of the house had known in what hour the thief was coming, he would have watched, and not allowed his house to be broken into. ⁴⁰ Therefore be ready also, for the Son of Man is coming in an hour that you don't expect him."* ⁴¹ Peter said to him, "Lord, are you telling this parable to us, or to everybody?" ⁴² The Lord said, *"Who then is the faithful and wise steward, whom his lord will set over his household, to give them their portion of food at the right times? ⁴³ Blessed is that servant whom his lord will find doing so when he comes. ⁴⁴ Truly I tell you, that he will set him over all that he has. ⁴⁵ But if that servant says in his heart, 'My lord delays his coming,' and begins to beat the menservants and the maidservants, and to eat and drink, and to be drunken, ⁴⁶ then the lord of that servant will come in a day when he isn't expecting him, and in an hour that he doesn't know, and will cut him in two, and place his portion with the unfaithful. ⁴⁷ That servant, who knew his lord's will, and didn't prepare, nor do what he wanted, will be beaten with many stripes, ⁴⁸ but he who didn't know, and did things worthy of stripes, will be beaten with few stripes. To whomever much is given, of him will much be required; and to whom much was entrusted, of him more will be asked.*

Not Peace but Division
  • **Luke 12: 49-53**

⁴⁹ *"I came to throw fire on the earth. I wish it were already kindled. ⁵⁰ But I have a baptism to be baptized with, and how distressed I am until it is accomplished! ⁵¹ Do you think that I have come to give peace in the earth? I tell you, no, but rather division. ⁵² For from now on, there will be five in one house divided, three against two, and two against three. ⁵³ They will be divided, father against son, and son against father; mother against daughter, and daughter against her mother; mother-in-law against her daughter-in-law, and daughter-in-law against her mother-in-law."*

Interpreting the End Times
- ### Luke 12: 54-59

[54] He said to the multitudes also, "When you see a cloud rising from the west, immediately you say, 'A shower is coming,' and so it happens. [55] When a south wind blows, you say, 'There will be a scorching heat,' and it happens. [56] You hypocrites! You know how to interpret the appearance of the earth and the sky, but how is it that you don't interpret this time? [57] Why don't you judge for yourselves what is right? [58] For when you are going with your adversary before the magistrate, try diligently on the way to be released from him, lest perhaps he drag you to the judge, and the judge deliver you to the officer, and the officer throw you into prison. [59] I tell you, you will by no means get out of there, until you have paid the very last penny."

Repent or Perish
- ### Luke 13: 1-9

[1] Now there were some present at the same time who told him about the Galileans, whose blood Pilate had mixed with their sacrifices. [2] Jesus answered them, *"Do you think that these Galileans were worse sinners than all the other Galileans, because they suffered such things? [3] I tell you, no, but unless you repent, you will all perish in the same way. [4] Or those eighteen, on whom the tower in Siloam fell, and killed them; do you think that they were worse offenders than all the men who dwell in Jerusalem? [5] I tell you, no, but, unless you repent, you will all perish in the same way."* [6] He spoke this parable. *"A certain man had a fig tree planted in his vineyard, and he came seeking fruit on it, and found none. [7] He said to the vine dresser, 'Behold, these three years I have come looking for fruit on this fig tree, and found none. Cut it down. Why does it waste the soil?' [8] He answered, 'Lord, leave it alone this year also, until I dig around it, and fertilize it. [9] If it bears fruit, fine; but if not, after that, you can cut it down.'"*

A Woman is Healed on the Sabbath
- ### Luke 13: 10-17

[10] He was teaching in one of the synagogues on the Sabbath day. [11] Behold, there was a woman who had a spirit of infirmity eighteen

years, and she was bent over, and could in no way straighten herself up. ¹²When Jesus saw her, he called her, and said to her, *"Woman, you are freed from your infirmity."* ¹³He laid his hands on her, and immediately she stood up straight, and glorified God. ¹⁴The ruler of the synagogue, being indignant because Jesus had healed on the Sabbath, said to the multitude, "There are six days in which men ought to work. Therefore come on those days and be healed, and not on the Sabbath day!" ¹⁵Therefore the Lord answered him, *"You hypocrites! Doesn't each one of you free his ox or his donkey from the stall on the Sabbath, and lead him away to water? ¹⁶Ought not this woman, being a daughter of Abraham, whom Satan had bound eighteen long years, be freed from this bondage on the Sabbath day?"* ¹⁷As he said these things, all his adversaries were disappointed, and all the multitude rejoiced for all the glorious things that were done by him.

The Narrow Door
- **Luke 13: 22-30**

²²He went on his way through cities and villages, teaching, and traveling on to Jerusalem. ²³One said to him, "Lord, are they few who are saved?" He said to them, ²⁴*"Strive to enter in by the narrow door, for many, I tell you, will seek to enter in, and will not be able. ²⁵When once the master of the house has risen up, and has shut the door, and you begin to stand outside, and to knock at the door, saying, 'Lord, Lord, open to us!' then he will answer and tell you, 'I don't know you or where you come from.' ²⁶Then you will begin to say, 'We ate and drank in your presence, and you taught in our streets.' ²⁷He will say, 'I tell you, I don't know where you come from. Depart from me, all you workers of iniquity.' ²⁸There will be weeping and gnashing of teeth, when you see Abraham, Isaac, Jacob, and all the prophets, in the Kingdom of God, and yourselves being thrown outside. ²⁹They will come from the east, west, north, and south, and will sit down in the Kingdom of God. ³⁰Behold, there are some who are last who will be first, and there are some who are first who will be last."*

At the Home of a Pharisee
- **Luke 14: 1-6**

¹ It happened, when he went into the house of one of the rulers of the Pharisees on a Sabbath to eat bread, that they were watching him. ² Behold, a certain man who had dropsy was in front of him. ³ Jesus, answering, spoke to the lawyers and Pharisees, saying, *"Is it lawful to heal on the Sabbath?"* ⁴ But they were silent. He took him, and healed him, and let him go. ⁵ He answered them, *"Which of you, if your son or an ox fell into a well, wouldn't immediately pull him out on a Sabbath day?"* ⁶ They couldn't answer him regarding these things.

Humility
- **Luke 14: 7-14**

⁷ He spoke a parable to those who were invited, when he noticed how they chose the best seats, and said to them, ⁸ *"When you are invited by anyone to a marriage feast, don't sit in the best seat, since perhaps someone more honorable than you might be invited by him,* ⁹ *and he who invited both of you would come and tell you, 'Make room for this person.' Then you would begin, with shame, to take the lowest place.* ¹⁰ *But when you are invited, go and sit in the lowest place, so that when he who invited you comes, he may tell you, 'Friend, move up higher.' Then you will be honored in the presence of all who sit at the table with you.* ¹¹ *For everyone who exalts himself will be humbled, and whoever humbles himself will be exalted."* ¹² He also said to the one who had invited him, *"When you make a dinner or a supper, don't call your friends, nor your brothers, nor your kinsmen, nor rich neighbors, or perhaps they might also return the favor, and pay you back.* ¹³ *But when you make a feast, ask the poor, the maimed, the lame, or the blind;* ¹⁴ *and you will be blessed, because they don't have the resources to repay you. For you will be repaid in the resurrection of the righteous."*

The Great Banquet
- **Luke 14: 15-24**

¹⁵ When one of those who sat at the table with him heard these things, he said to him, "Blessed is he who will feast in the Kingdom

of God!" [16] But he said to him, *"A certain man made a great supper, and he invited many people.* [17] *He sent out his servant at supper time to tell those who were invited, 'Come, for everything is ready now.'* [18] *They all as one began to make excuses. "The first said to him, 'I have bought a field, and I must go and see it. Please have me excused.'* [19] *"Another said, 'I have bought five yoke of oxen, and I must go try them out. Please have me excused.'* [20] *"Another said, 'I have married a wife, and therefore I can't come.'* [21] *"That servant came, and told his lord these things. Then the master of the house, being angry, said to his servant, 'Go out quickly into the streets and lanes of the city, and bring in the poor, maimed, blind, and lame.'* [22] *"The servant said, 'Lord, it is done as you commanded, and there is still room.'* [23] *"The lord said to the servant, 'Go out into the highways and hedges, and compel them to come in, that my house may be filled.* [24] *For I tell you that none of those men who were invited will taste of my supper.'"*

The Cost of Becoming a Disciple
  • **Luke 14: 25-35**
[25] Now great multitudes were going with him. He turned and said to them, [26] *"If anyone comes to me, and doesn't disregard his own father, mother, wife, children, brothers, and sisters, yes, and his own life also, he can't be my disciple.* [27] *Whoever doesn't bear his own cross, and come after me, can't be my disciple.* [28] *For which of you, desiring to build a tower, doesn't first sit down and count the cost, to see if he has enough to complete it?* [29] *Or perhaps, when he has laid a foundation, and is not able to finish, everyone who sees begins to mock him,* [30] *saying, 'This man began to build, and wasn't able to finish.'* [31] *Or what king, as he goes to encounter another king in war, will not sit down first and consider whether he is able with ten thousand to meet him who comes against him with twenty thousand?* [32] *Or else, while the other is yet a great way off, he sends an envoy, and asks for conditions of peace.* [33] *So therefore whoever of you who doesn't renounce all that he has, he can't be my disciple.* [34] *Salt is good, but if the salt becomes flat and tasteless, with what do you season it?* [35] *It is fit neither for the soil nor for the manure pile. It is thrown out. He who has ears to hear, let him hear."*

The Lost Sheep
* ### Luke 15: 1-7 (Matthew 18: 12-14)

[1] Now all the tax collectors and sinners were coming close to him to hear him. [2] The Pharisees and the scribes murmured, saying, "This man welcomes sinners, and eats with them." [3] He told them this parable. [4] *"Which of you men, if you had one hundred sheep, and lost one of them, wouldn't leave the ninety-nine in the wilderness, and go after the one that was lost, until he found it?* [5] *When he has found it, he carries it on his shoulders, rejoicing.* [6] *When he comes home, he calls together his friends and his neighbors, saying to them, 'Rejoice with me, for I have found my sheep which was lost!'* [7] *I tell you that even so there will be more joy in heaven over one sinner who repents, than over ninety-nine righteous people who need no repentance.*

The Lost Coin
* ### Luke 15: 8-10

[8] *Or what woman, if she had ten drachma coins, if she lost one drachma coin, wouldn't light a lamp, sweep the house, and seek diligently until she found it?* [9] *When she has found it, she calls together her friends and neighbors, saying, 'Rejoice with me, for I have found the drachma which I had lost.'* [10] *Even so, I tell you, there is joy in the presence of the angels of God over one sinner repenting."*

The Lost Son
* ### Luke 15: 11-32

[11] He said, *"A certain man had two sons.* [12] *The younger of them said to his father, 'Father, give me my share of your property.' He divided his livelihood between them.* [13] *Not many days after, the younger son gathered all of this together and traveled into a far country. There he wasted his property with riotous living.* [14] *When he had spent all of it, there arose a severe famine in that country, and he began to be in need.* [15] *He went and joined himself to one of the citizens of that country, and he sent him into his fields to feed pigs.* [16] *He wanted to fill his belly with the husks that the pigs ate, but no one gave him any.* [17] *But when he came to himself he said, 'How many hired servants of my father's have bread enough to spare, and I'm dying with hunger!* [18] *I will get up and go to my father, and will tell him, "Father, I have*

sinned against heaven, and in your sight. [19] *I am no more worthy to be called your son. Make me as one of your hired servants."'* [20] *"He arose, and came to his father. But while he was still far off, his father saw him, and was moved with compassion, and ran, and fell on his neck, and kissed him.* [21] *The son said to him, 'Father, I have sinned against heaven, and in your sight. I am no longer worthy to be called your son.'* [22] *"But the father said to his servants, 'Bring out the best robe, and put it on him. Put a ring on his hand, and shoes on his feet.* [23] *Bring the fattened calf, kill it, and let us eat, and celebrate;* [24] *for this, my son, was dead, and is alive again. He was lost, and is found.' They began to celebrate.* [25] *"Now his elder son was in the field. As he came near to the house, he heard music and dancing.* [26] *He called one of the servants to him, and asked what was going on.* [27] *He said to him, 'Your brother has come, and your father has killed the fattened calf, because he has received him back safe and healthy.'* [28] *But he was angry, and would not go in. Therefore his father came out, and begged him.* [29] *But he answered his father, 'Behold, these many years I have served you, and I never disobeyed a commandment of yours, but you never gave me a goat, that I might celebrate with my friends.* [30] *But when this, your son, came, who has devoured your living with prostitutes, you killed the fattened calf for him.'* [31] *"He said to him, 'Son, you are always with me, and all that is mine is yours.* [32] *But it was appropriate to celebrate and be glad, for this, your brother, was dead, and is alive again. He was lost, and is found.'"*

The Wise Manager
• Luke 16: 1-15

[1] He also said to his disciples, *"There was a certain rich man who had a manager. An accusation was made to him that this man was wasting his possessions.* [2] *He called him, and said to him, 'What is this that I hear about you? Give an accounting of your management, for you can no longer be manager.'* [3] *"The manager said within himself, 'What will I do, seeing that my lord is taking away the management position from me? I don't have strength to dig. I am ashamed to beg.* [4] *I know what I will do, so that when I am removed from management, they may receive me into their houses.'* [5] *Calling each*

one of his lord's debtors to him, he said to the first, 'How much do you owe to my lord?' ⁶ He said, 'A hundred batos of oil.' He said to him, 'Take your bill, and sit down quickly and write fifty.' ⁷ Then he said to another, 'How much do you owe?' He said, 'A hundred cors of wheat.' He said to him, 'Take your bill, and write eighty.' ⁸ "His lord commended the dishonest manager because he had done wisely, for the children of this world are, in their own generation, wiser than the children of the light. ⁹ I tell you, make for yourselves friends by means of unrighteous mammon, so that when you fail, they may receive you into the eternal tents. ¹⁰ He who is faithful in a very little is faithful also in much. He who is dishonest in a very little is also dishonest in much. ¹¹ If therefore you have not been faithful in the unrighteous mammon, who will commit to your trust the true riches? ¹² If you have not been faithful in that which is another's, who will give you that which is your own? ¹³ No servant can serve two masters, for either he will hate the one, and love the other; or else he will hold to one, and despise the other. You aren't able to serve God and mammon." ¹⁴ The Pharisees, who were lovers of money, also heard all these things, and they scoffed at him. ¹⁵ He said to them, *"You are those who justify yourselves in the sight of men, but God knows your hearts. For that which is exalted among men is an abomination in the sight of God.*

The Rich Man and the Beggar
• Luke 16: 19-31

¹⁹ "Now there was a certain rich man, and he was clothed in purple and fine linen, living in luxury every day. ²⁰ A certain beggar, named Lazarus, was laid at his gate, full of sores, ²¹ and desiring to be fed with the crumbs that fell from the rich man's table. Yes, even the dogs came and licked his sores. ²² It happened that the beggar died, and that he was carried away by the angels to Abraham's bosom. The rich man also died, and was buried. ²³ In Hades, he lifted up his eyes, being in torment, and saw Abraham far off, and Lazarus at his bosom. ²⁴ He cried and said, 'Father Abraham, have mercy on me, and send Lazarus, that he may dip the tip of his finger in water, and cool my tongue! For I am in anguish in this flame.' ²⁵ "But Abraham said, 'Son, remember that you, in your lifetime, received your good things, and Lazarus, in the same way, bad things. But now here he is comforted and you are in anguish. [26] Besides all this, between us and you there is a great gulf fixed, that those who want to pass from here to you are not able, and that none may cross over from there to us.' [27] *"He said, 'I ask you therefore, father, that you would send him to my father's house; [28] for I have five brothers, that he may testify to them, so they won't also come into this place of torment.'* [29] *"But Abraham said to him, 'They have Moses and the prophets. Let them listen to them.'* [30] *"He said, 'No, father Abraham, but if one goes to them from the dead, they will repent.'* [31] *"He said to him, 'If they don't listen to Moses and the prophets, neither will they be persuaded if one rises from the dead.'"*

Sin, Faith, and Duty
  • **Luke 17: 5-10**
[5] The apostles said to the Lord, "Increase our faith." [6] The Lord said, *"If you had faith like a grain of mustard seed, you would tell this sycamore tree, 'Be uprooted, and be planted in the sea,' and it would obey you. [7] But who is there among you, having a servant plowing or keeping sheep, that will say, when he comes in from the field, 'Come immediately and sit down at the table,' [8] and will not rather tell him, 'Prepare my supper, clothe yourself properly, and serve me, while I eat and drink. Afterward you shall eat and drink'? [9] Does he thank that servant because he did the things that were commanded? I think not. [10] Even so you also, when you have done all the things that are commanded you, say, 'We are unworthy servants. We have done our duty.'"*

Jesus Heals Ten Lepers
  • **Luke 17: 11-19**
[11] It happened as he was on his way to Jerusalem, that he was passing along the borders of Samaria and Galilee. [12] As he entered into a certain village, ten men who were lepers met him, who stood at a distance. [13] They lifted up their voices, saying, "Jesus, Master, have mercy on us!" [14] When he saw them, he said to them, *"Go and show yourselves to the priests."* It happened that as they went, they were cleansed. [15] One of them, when he saw that he was healed,

turned back, glorifying God with a loud voice. [16] He fell on his face at Jesus' feet, giving him thanks; and he was a Samaritan. [17] Jesus answered, *"Weren't the ten cleansed? But where are the nine? [18] Were there none found who returned to give glory to God, except this stranger?"* [19] Then he said to him, *"Get up, and go your way. Your faith has healed you."*

The Kingdom of God
* **Luke 17: 20-37**

[20] Being asked by the Pharisees when the Kingdom of God would come, he answered them, *"The Kingdom of God doesn't come with observation; [21] neither will they say, 'Look, here!' or, 'Look, there!' for behold, the Kingdom of God is within you."* [22] He said to the disciples, *"The days will come, when you will desire to see one of the days of the Son of Man, and you will not see it. [23] They will tell you, 'Look, here!' or 'Look, there!' Don't go away, nor follow after them, [24] for as the lightning, when it flashes out of the one part under the sky, shines to the other part under the sky; so will the Son of Man be in his day. [25] But first, he must suffer many things and be rejected by this generation. [26] As it happened in the days of Noah, even so will it be also in the days of the Son of Man. [27] They ate, they drank, they married, they were given in marriage, until the day that Noah entered into the ship, and the flood came, and destroyed them all. [28] Likewise, even as it happened in the days of Lot: they ate, they drank, they bought, they sold, they planted, they built; [29] but in the day that Lot went out from Sodom, it rained fire and sulfur from the sky, and destroyed them all. [30] It will be the same way in the day that the Son of Man is revealed. [31] In that day, he who will be on the housetop, and his goods in the house, let him not go down to take them away. Let him who is in the field likewise not turn back. [32] Remember Lot's wife! [33] Whoever seeks to save his life loses it, but whoever loses his life preserves it. [34] I tell you, in that night there will be two people in one bed. The one will be taken, and the other will be left. [35] There will be two grinding grain together. One will be taken, and the other will be left."* [36-37] They, answering, asked him, "Where, Lord?" He said to them, *"Where the body is, there will the vultures also be gathered together."*

The Persistent Widow
- ## Luke 18: 1-8

[1] He also spoke a parable to them that they must always pray, and not give up, [2] saying, *"There was a judge in a certain city who didn't fear God, and didn't respect man. [3] A widow was in that city, and she often came to him, saying, 'Defend me from my adversary!' [4] He wouldn't for a while, but afterward he said to himself, 'Though I neither fear God, nor respect man, [5] yet because this widow bothers me, I will defend her, or else she will wear me out by her continual coming.'" [6] The Lord said, "Listen to what the unrighteous judge says. [7] Won't God avenge his chosen ones, who are crying out to him day and night, and yet he exercises patience with them? [8] I tell you that he will avenge them quickly. Nevertheless, when the Son of Man comes, will he find faith on the earth?"*

The Pharisee and the Tax Collector
- ## Luke 18: 9-14

[9] He spoke also this parable to certain people who were convinced of their own righteousness, and who despised all others. [10] *"Two men went up into the temple to pray; one was a Pharisee, and the other was a tax collector. [11] The Pharisee stood and prayed to himself like this: 'God, I thank you, that I am not like the rest of men, extortioners, unrighteous, adulterers, or even like this tax collector. [12] I fast twice a week. I give tithes of all that I get.' [13] But the tax collector, standing far away, wouldn't even lift up his eyes to heaven, but beat his breast, saying, 'God, be merciful to me, a sinner!' [14] I tell you, this man went down to his house justified rather than the other; for everyone who exalts himself will be humbled, but he who humbles himself will be exalted."*

Marriage and Divorce
- ## Matthew 19: 1-12 (Mark 10: 1-12)

[1] It happened when Jesus had finished these words, he departed from Galilee, and came into the borders of Judea beyond the Jordan. [2] Great multitudes followed him, and he healed them there. [3] Pharisees came to him, testing him, and saying, "Is it lawful for a man to divorce his wife for any reason?" [4] He answered, *"Haven't you read that he who*

made them from the beginning made them male and female, ⁵ *and said, 'For this cause a man shall leave his father and mother, and shall join to his wife; and the two shall become one flesh?'* ⁶ *So that they are no more two, but one flesh. What therefore God has joined together, don't let man tear apart."* ⁷ They asked him, "Why then did Moses command us to give her a bill of divorce, and divorce her?" ⁸ He said to them, *"Moses, because of the hardness of your hearts, allowed you to divorce your wives, but from the beginning it has not been so.* ⁹ *I tell you that whoever divorces his wife, except for sexual immorality, and marries another, commits adultery; and he who marries her when she is divorced commits adultery."* ¹⁰ His disciples said to him, "If this is the case of the man with his wife, it is not expedient to marry." ¹¹ But he said to them, *"Not all men can receive this saying, but those to whom it is given.* ¹² *For there are eunuchs who were born that way from their mother's womb, and there are eunuchs who were made eunuchs by men; and there are eunuchs who made themselves eunuchs for the Kingdom of Heaven's sake. He who is able to receive it, let him receive it."*

Jesus Blesses the Children
- **Mark 10: 13-16 (Matthew 19: 13-15; Luke 18: 15-17)**

¹³ They were bringing to him little children, that he should touch them, but the disciples rebuked those who were bringing them. ¹⁴ But when Jesus saw it, he was moved with indignation, and said to them, *"Allow the little children to come to me! Don't forbid them, for the Kingdom of God belongs to such as these.* ¹⁵ *Most certainly I tell you, whoever will not receive the Kingdom of God like a little child, he will in no way enter into it."* ¹⁶ He took them in his arms, and blessed them, laying his hands on them.

The Rich Young Ruler
- **Matthew 19: 16-30 (Mark 10: 17-31; Luke 18: 18-30)**

¹⁶ Behold, one came to him and said, "Good teacher, what good thing shall I do, that I may have eternal life?" ¹⁷ He said to him, *"Why do you call me good? No one is good but one, that is, God. But if you want to enter into life, keep the commandments."* ¹⁸ He said to him, "Which ones?" Jesus said, "'You shall not murder.' 'You shall not

commit adultery.' 'You shall not steal.' 'You shall not offer false testimony.' *[19]* 'Honor your father and mother.' And, 'You shall love your neighbor as yourself.'"* *[20]* The young man said to him, "All these things I have observed from my youth. What do I still lack?" *[21]* Jesus said to him, *"If you want to be perfect, go, sell what you have, and give to the poor, and you will have treasure in heaven; and come, follow me."* *[22]* But when the young man heard the saying, he went away sad, for he was one who had great possessions. *[23]* Jesus said to his disciples, *"Most certainly I say to you, a rich man will enter into the Kingdom of Heaven with difficulty. *[24]* Again I tell you, it is easier for a camel to go through a needle's eye, than for a rich man to enter into the Kingdom of God."* *[25]* When the disciples heard it, they were exceedingly astonished, saying, "Who then can be saved?" *[26]* Looking at them, Jesus said, *"With men this is impossible, but with God all things are possible."* *[27]* Then Peter answered, "Behold, we have left everything, and followed you. What then will we have?" *[28]* Jesus said to them, *"Most certainly I tell you that you who have followed me, in the regeneration when the Son of Man will sit on the throne of his glory, you also will sit on twelve thrones, judging the twelve tribes of Israel. *[29]* Everyone who has left houses, or brothers, or sisters, or father, or mother, or wife, or children, or lands, for my name's sake, will receive one hundred times, and will inherit eternal life. *[30]* But many will be last who are first; and first who are last.*

The Vineyard Workers
• Matthew 20: 1-16

[1] *"For the Kingdom of Heaven is like a man who was the master of a household, who went out early in the morning to hire laborers for his vineyard. *[2]* When he had agreed with the laborers for a denarius a day, he sent them into his vineyard. *[3]* He went out about the third hour, and saw others standing idle in the marketplace. *[4]* To them he said, 'You also go into the vineyard, and whatever is right I will give you.' So they went their way. *[5]* Again he went out about the sixth and the ninth hour, and did likewise. *[6]* About the eleventh hour he went out, and found others standing idle. He said to them, 'Why do you stand here all day idle?' *[7]* "They said to him, 'Because no one has hired us.' "He said to them, 'You also go into the vineyard, and*

you will receive whatever is right.' [8] *When evening had come, the lord of the vineyard said to his manager, 'Call the laborers and pay them their wages, beginning from the last to the first.'* [9] *"When those who were hired at about the eleventh hour came, they each received a denarius.* [10] *When the first came, they supposed that they would receive more; and they likewise each received a denarius.* [11] *When they received it, they murmured against the master of the household,* [12] *saying, 'These last have spent one hour, and you have made them equal to us, who have borne the burden of the day and the scorching heat!'* [13] *"But he answered one of them, 'Friend, I am doing you no wrong. Didn't you agree with me for a denarius?* [14] *Take that which is yours, and go your way. It is my desire to give to this last just as much as to you.* [15] *Isn't it lawful for me to do what I want to with what I own? Or is your eye evil, because I am good?'* [16] *So the last will be first, and the first last. For many are called, but few are chosen."*

Jesus Predicts His Death a Third Time
   • **Luke 18: 31-34 (Matthew 20: 17-19; Mark 10: 32-34)**
[31] He took the twelve aside, and said to them, *"Behold, we are going up to Jerusalem, and all the things that are written through the prophets concerning the Son of Man will be completed.* [32] *For he will be delivered up to the Gentiles, will be mocked, treated shamefully, and spit on.* [33] *They will scourge and kill him. On the third day, he will rise again."* [34] They understood none of these things. This saying was hidden from them, and they didn't understand the things that were said.

Serving Others
   • **Matthew 20: 20-28 (Mark 10: 35-45)**
[20] Then the mother of the sons of Zebedee came to him with her sons, kneeling and asking a certain thing of him. [21] He said to her, *"What do you want?"* She said to him, "Command that these, my two sons, may sit, one on your right hand, and one on your left hand, in your Kingdom." [22] But Jesus answered, *"You don't know what you are asking. Are you able to drink the cup that I am about to drink, and be baptized with the baptism that I am baptized with?"* They said to him, "We are able." [23] He said to them, *"You will indeed drink my*

cup, and be baptized with the baptism that I am baptized with, but to sit on my right hand and on my left hand is not mine to give; but it is for whom it has been prepared by my Father." [24] When the ten heard it, they were indignant with the two brothers. [25] But Jesus summoned them, and said, *"You know that the rulers of the nations lord it over them, and their great ones exercise authority over them.* [26] *It shall not be so among you, but whoever desires to become great among you shall be your servant.* [27] *Whoever desires to be first among you shall be your bondservant,* [28] *even as the Son of Man came not to be served, but to serve, and to give his life as a ransom for many."*

A Blind Beggar Receives His Sight
• Mark 10: 46-52 (Matthew 20: 29-34; Luke 18: 35-43)

[46] They came to Jericho. As he went out from Jericho, with his disciples and a great multitude, the son of Timaeus, Bartimaeus, a blind beggar, was sitting by the road. [47] When he heard that it was Jesus the Nazarene, he began to cry out, and say, "Jesus, you son of David, have mercy on me!" [48] Many rebuked him, that he should be quiet, but he cried out much more, "You son of David, have mercy on me!" [49] Jesus stood still, and said, *"Call him."* They called the blind man, saying to him, "Cheer up! Get up. He is calling you!" [50] He, casting away his cloak, sprang up, and came to Jesus. [51] Jesus asked him, *"What do you want me to do for you?"* The blind man said to him, "Rabboni, that I may see again." [52] Jesus said to him, *"Go your way. Your faith has made you well."* Immediately he received his sight, and followed Jesus on the way.

The Tax Collector
• Luke 19: 1-10

[1] He entered and was passing through Jericho. [2] There was a man named Zacchaeus. He was a chief tax collector, and he was rich. [3] He was trying to see who Jesus was, and couldn't because of the crowd, because he was short. [4] He ran on ahead, and climbed up into a sycamore tree to see him, for he was to pass that way. [5] When Jesus came to the place, he looked up and saw him, and said to him, *"Zacchaeus, hurry and come down, for today I must stay at your house."* [6] He hurried, came down, and received him joyfully. [7] When

they saw it, they all murmured, saying, "He has gone in to lodge with a man who is a sinner." [8] Zacchaeus stood and said to the Lord, "Behold, Lord, half of my goods I give to the poor. If I have wrongfully exacted anything of anyone, I restore four times as much." [9] Jesus said to him, *"Today, salvation has come to this house, because he also is a son of Abraham. [10] For the Son of Man came to seek and to save that which was lost."*

The Ten Coins
   • **Luke 19: 11-27**

[11] As they heard these things, he went on and told a parable, because he was near Jerusalem, and they supposed that the Kingdom of God would be revealed immediately. [12] He said therefore, *"A certain nobleman went into a far country to receive for himself a kingdom, and to return. [13] He called ten servants of his, and gave them ten mina coins, and told them, 'Conduct business until I come.' [14] But his citizens hated him, and sent an envoy after him, saying, 'We don't want this man to reign over us.' [15] "It happened when he had come back again, having received the kingdom, that he commanded these servants, to whom he had given the money, to be called to him, that he might know what they had gained by conducting business. [16] The first came before him, saying, 'Lord, your mina has made ten more minas.' [17] "He said to him, 'Well done, you good servant! Because you were found faithful with very little, you shall have authority over ten cities.' [18] "The second came, saying, 'Your mina, Lord, has made five minas.' [19] "So he said to him, 'And you are to be over five cities.' [20] Another came, saying, 'Lord, behold, your mina, which I kept laid away in a handkerchief, [21] for I feared you, because you are an exacting man. You take up that which you didn't lay down, and reap that which you didn't sow.' [22] "He said to him, 'Out of your own mouth will I judge you, you wicked servant! You knew that I am an exacting man, taking up that which I didn't lay down, and reaping that which I didn't sow. [23] Then why didn't you deposit my money in the bank, and at my coming, I might have earned interest on it?' [24] He said to those who stood by, 'Take the mina away from him, and give it to him who has the ten minas.' [25] "They said to him, 'Lord, he has ten minas!' [26] 'For I tell you that to everyone who has, will more*

111

be given; but from him who doesn't have, even that which he has will be taken away from him. ²⁷ *But bring those enemies of mine who didn't want me to reign over them here, and kill them before me.'"*

The Death and Resurrection of Lazarus
• **John 11: 1-44**

¹ Now a certain man was sick, Lazarus from Bethany, of the village of Mary and her sister, Martha. ² It was that Mary who had anointed the Lord with ointment, and wiped his feet with her hair, whose brother, Lazarus, was sick. ³ The sisters therefore sent to him, saying, "Lord, behold, he for whom you have great affection is sick." ⁴ But when Jesus heard it, he said, *"This sickness is not to death, but for the glory of God, that God's Son may be glorified by it."* ⁵ Now Jesus loved Martha, and her sister, and Lazarus. ⁶ When therefore he heard that he was sick, he stayed two days in the place where he was. ⁷ Then after this he said to the disciples, *"Let's go into Judea again."* ⁸ The disciples told him, "Rabbi, the Jews were just trying to stone you, and are you going there again?" ⁹ Jesus answered, *"Aren't there twelve hours of daylight? If a man walks in the day, he doesn't stumble, because he sees the light of this world.* ¹⁰ *But if a man walks in the night, he stumbles, because the light isn't in him."* ¹¹ He said these things, and after that, he said to them, *"Our friend, Lazarus, has fallen asleep, but I am going so that I may awake him out of sleep."* ¹² The disciples therefore said, "Lord, if he has fallen asleep, he will recover." ¹³ Now Jesus had spoken of his death, but they thought that he spoke of taking rest in sleep. ¹⁴ So Jesus said to them plainly then, *"Lazarus is dead.* ¹⁵ *I am glad for your sakes that I was not there, so that you may believe. Nevertheless, let's go to him."* ¹⁶ Thomas therefore, who is called Didymus, said to his fellow disciples, "Let's go also, that we may die with him." ¹⁷ So when Jesus came, he found that he had been in the tomb four days already. ¹⁸ Now Bethany was near Jerusalem, about fifteen stadia away. ¹⁹ Many of the Jews had joined the women around Martha and Mary, to console them concerning their brother. ²⁰ Then when Martha heard that Jesus was coming, she went and met him, but Mary stayed in the house. ²¹ Therefore Martha said to Jesus, "Lord, if you would have been here, my brother wouldn't have died. ²² Even now I know

that, whatever you ask of God, God will give you." [23] Jesus said to her, *"Your brother will rise again."* [24] Martha said to him, "I know that he will rise again in the resurrection at the last day." [25] Jesus said to her, *"I am the resurrection and the life. He who believes in me will still live, even if he dies. [26] Whoever lives and believes in me will never die. Do you believe this?"* [27] She said to him, "Yes, Lord. I have come to believe that you are the Christ, God's Son, he who comes into the world." [28] When she had said this, she went away, and called Mary, her sister, secretly, saying, "The Teacher is here, and is calling you." [29] When she heard this, she arose quickly, and went to him. [30] Now Jesus had not yet come into the village, but was in the place where Martha met him. [31] Then the Jews who were with her in the house, and were consoling her, when they saw Mary, that she rose up quickly and went out, followed her, saying, "She is going to the tomb to weep there." [32] Therefore when Mary came to where Jesus was, and saw him, she fell down at his feet, saying to him, "Lord, if you would have been here, my brother wouldn't have died." [33] When Jesus therefore saw her weeping, and the Jews weeping who came with her, he groaned in the spirit, and was troubled, [34] and said, *"Where have you laid him?"* They told him, "Lord, come and see." [35] Jesus wept. [36] The Jews therefore said, "See how much affection he had for him!" [37] Some of them said, "Couldn't this man, who opened the eyes of him who was blind, have also kept this man from dying?" [38] Jesus therefore, again groaning in himself, came to the tomb. Now it was a cave, and a stone lay against it. [39] Jesus said, *"Take away the stone."* Martha, the sister of him who was dead, said to him, "Lord, by this time there is a stench, for he has been dead four days." [40] Jesus said to her, *"Didn't I tell you that if you believed, you would see God's glory?"* [41] So they took away the stone from the place where the dead man was lying. Jesus lifted up his eyes, and said, *"Father, I thank you that you listened to me. [42] I know that you always listen to me, but because of the multitude that stands around I said this, that they may believe that you sent me."* [43] When he had said this, he cried with a loud voice, *"Lazarus, come out!"* [44] He who was dead came out, bound hand and foot with wrappings, and his face was wrapped around with a cloth. Jesus said to them, *"Free him, and let him go."*

A Plot to Kill Jesus
- **John 11: 45-57 (Matthew 26: 1-5; Mark 14: 1-2; Luke 22: 1-2)**

[45] Therefore many of the Jews, who came to Mary and saw what Jesus did, believed in him. [46] But some of them went away to the Pharisees, and told them the things which Jesus had done. [47] The chief priests therefore and the Pharisees gathered a council, and said, "What are we doing? For this man does many signs. [48] If we leave him alone like this, everyone will believe in him, and the Romans will come and take away both our place and our nation." [49] But a certain one of them, Caiaphas, being high priest that year, said to them, "You know nothing at all, [50] nor do you consider that it is advantageous for us that one man should die for the people, and that the whole nation not perish." [51] Now he didn't say this of himself, but being high priest that year, he prophesied that Jesus would die for the nation, [52] and not for the nation only, but that he might also gather together into one the children of God who are scattered abroad. [53] So from that day forward they took counsel that they might put him to death. [54] Jesus therefore walked no more openly among the Jews, but departed from there into the country near the wilderness, to a city called Ephraim. He stayed there with his disciples. [55] Now the Passover of the Jews was at hand. Many went up from the country to Jerusalem before the Passover, to purify themselves. [56] Then they sought for Jesus and spoke one with another, as they stood in the temple, "What do you think—that he isn't coming to the feast at all?" [57] Now the chief priests and the Pharisees had commanded that if anyone knew where he was, he should report it, that they might seize him.

Jesus is Anointed at Bethany
- **John 12: 1-11 (Matthew 26: 6-13; Mark 14: 3-9)**

[1] Then six days before the Passover, Jesus came to Bethany, where Lazarus was, who had been dead, whom he raised from the dead. [2] So they made him a supper there. Martha served, but Lazarus was one of those who sat at the table with him. [3] Mary, therefore, took a pound of ointment of pure nard, very precious, and anointed the feet of Jesus, and wiped his feet with her hair. The house was filled

with the fragrance of the ointment. ⁴Then Judas Iscariot, Simon's son, one of his disciples, who would betray him, said, ⁵"Why wasn't this ointment sold for three hundred denarii, and given to the poor?" ⁶Now he said this, not because he cared for the poor, but because he was a thief, and having the money box, used to steal what was put into it. ⁷But Jesus said, *"Leave her alone. She has kept this for the day of my burial. ⁸For you always have the poor with you, but you don't always have me."* ⁹A large crowd therefore of the Jews learned that he was there, and they came, not for Jesus' sake only, but that they might see Lazarus also, whom he had raised from the dead. ¹⁰But the chief priests conspired to put Lazarus to death also, ¹¹because on account of him many of the Jews went away and believed in Jesus.

Judas Agrees to Betray Jesus
- **Luke 22: 3-6 (Matthew 26: 14-16; Mark 14: 10-11)**

³Satan entered into Judas, who was also called Iscariot, who was numbered with the twelve. ⁴He went away, and talked with the chief priests and captains about how he might deliver him to them. ⁵They were glad, and agreed to give him money. ⁶He consented, and sought an opportunity to deliver him to them in the absence of the multitude.

Jesus Enters Jerusalem
- **Matthew 21: 1-11 (Mark 11: 1-11; Luke 19: 28-44; John 12: 12-19)**

¹When they drew near to Jerusalem, and came to Bethsphage, to the Mount of Olives, then Jesus sent two disciples, ²saying to them, *"Go into the village that is opposite you, and immediately you will find a donkey tied, and a colt with her. Untie them, and bring them to me. ³If anyone says anything to you, you shall say, 'The Lord needs them,' and immediately he will send them."* ⁴All this was done, that it might be fulfilled which was spoken through the prophet, saying, ⁵"Tell the daughter of Zion, behold, your King comes to you, humble, and riding on a donkey, on a colt, the foal of a donkey." ⁶The disciples went, and did just as Jesus commanded them, ⁷and brought the donkey and the colt, and laid their clothes on them; and

he sat on them. [8]A very great multitude spread their clothes on the road. Others cut branches from the trees, and spread them on the road. [9]The multitudes who went before him, and who followed kept shouting, "Hosanna to the son of David! Blessed is he who comes in the name of the Lord! Hosanna in the highest!" [10]When he had come into Jerusalem, all the city was stirred up, saying, "Who is this?" [11] The multitudes said, "This is the prophet, Jesus, from Nazareth of Galilee."

The Fruitless Fig Tree
- ### Mark 11: 12-14 (Matthew 21: 18-19a)

[12]The next day, when they had come out from Bethany, he was hungry. [13]Seeing a fig tree afar off having leaves, he came to see if perhaps he might find anything on it. When he came to it, he found nothing but leaves, for it was not the season for figs. [14]Jesus told it, *"May no one ever eat fruit from you again!"* and his disciples heard it.

Jesus Clears the Temple Again
- ### Matthew 21: 12-17 (Mark 11: 15-19; Luke 19: 45-48)

[12]Jesus entered into the temple of God, and drove out all of those who sold and bought in the temple, and overthrew the money changers' tables and the seats of those who sold the doves. [13]He said to them, *"It is written, 'My house shall be called a house of prayer,' but you have made it a den of robbers!"* [14]The blind and the lame came to him in the temple, and he healed them. [15]But when the chief priests and the scribes saw the wonderful things that he did, and the children who were crying in the temple and saying, "Hosanna to the son of David!" they were indignant, [16]and said to him, "Do you hear what these are saying?" Jesus said to them, *"Yes. Did you never read, 'Out of the mouth of babes and nursing babies you have per- fected praise?'"* [17]He left them, and went out of the city to Bethany, and lodged there.

The Withered Fig Tree
- **Mark 11: 20-26 (Matthew 21: 19b-22)**

[20] As they passed by in the morning, they saw the fig tree withered away from the roots. [21] Peter, remembering, said to him, "Rabbi, look! The fig tree which you cursed has withered away." [22] Jesus answered them, *"Have faith in God. [23] For most certainly I tell you, whoever may tell this mountain, 'Be taken up and cast into the sea,' and doesn't doubt in his heart, but believes that what he says is happening; he shall have whatever he says. [24] Therefore I tell you, all things whatever you pray and ask for, believe that you have received them, and you shall have them. [25] Whenever you stand praying, forgive, if you have anything against anyone; so that your Father, who is in heaven, may also forgive you your transgressions. [26] But if you do not forgive, neither will your Father in heaven forgive your transgressions."*

The Purpose of Jesus' Death
- **John 12: 20-36**

[20] Now there were certain Greeks among those that went up to worship at the feast. [21] These, therefore, came to Philip, who was from Bethsaida of Galilee, and asked him, saying, "Sir, we want to see Jesus." [22] Philip came and told Andrew, and in turn, Andrew came with Philip, and they told Jesus. [23] Jesus answered them, *"The time has come for the Son of Man to be glorified. [24] Most certainly I tell you, unless a grain of wheat falls into the earth and dies, it remains by itself alone. But if it dies, it bears much fruit. [25] He who loves his life will lose it. He who hates his life in this world will keep it to eternal life. [26] If anyone serves me, let him follow me. Where I am, there will my servant also be. If anyone serves me, the Father will honor him. [27] "Now my soul is troubled. What shall I say? 'Father, save me from this time?' But for this cause I came to this time. [28] Father, glorify your name!"* Then there came a voice out of the sky, saying, "I have both glorified it, and will glorify it again." [29] The multitude therefore, who stood by and heard it, said that it had thundered. Others said, "An angel has spoken to him." [30] Jesus answered, *"This voice hasn't come for my sake, but for your sakes. [31] Now is the judgment of this world. Now the prince of this world will be cast*

out. ³² And I, if I am lifted up from the earth, will draw all people to myself." ³³ But he said this, signifying by what kind of death he should die. ³⁴ The multitude answered him, "We have heard out of the law that the Christ remains forever. How do you say, *'The Son of Man must be lifted up?'* Who is this Son of Man?" ³⁵ Jesus therefore said to them, *"Yet a little while the light is with you. Walk while you have the light, that darkness doesn't overtake you. He who walks in the darkness doesn't know where he is going. ³⁶ While you have the light, believe in the light, that you may become children of light."* Jesus said these things, and he departed and hid himself from them.

Unbelief Among the Jews
   • **John 12: 37-50**

³⁷ But though he had done so many signs before them, yet they didn't believe in him, ³⁸ that the word of Isaiah the prophet might be fulfilled, which he spoke, "Lord, who has believed our report? To whom has the arm of the Lord been revealed?" ³⁹ For this cause they couldn't believe, for Isaiah said again, ⁴⁰ "He has blinded their eyes and he hardened their heart, lest they should see with their eyes, and perceive with their heart, and would turn, and I would heal them." ⁴¹ Isaiah said these things when he saw his glory, and spoke of him. ⁴² Nevertheless even of the rulers many believed in him, but because of the Pharisees they didn't confess it, so that they wouldn't be put out of the synagogue, ⁴³ for they loved men's praise more than God's praise. ⁴⁴ Jesus cried out and said, *"Whoever believes in me, believes not in me, but in him who sent me. ⁴⁵ He who sees me sees him who sent me. ⁴⁶ I have come as a light into the world, that whoever believes in me may not remain in the darkness. ⁴⁷ If anyone listens to my sayings, and doesn't believe, I don't judge him. For I came not to judge the world, but to save the world. ⁴⁸ He who rejects me, and doesn't receive my sayings, has one who judges him. The word that I spoke, the same will judge him in the last day. ⁴⁹ For I spoke not from myself, but the Father who sent me, he gave me a commandment, what I should say, and what I should speak. ⁵⁰ I know that his commandment is eternal life. The things therefore which I speak, even as the Father has said to me, so I speak."*

The Authority of Jesus is Questioned
- **Mark 11: 27-33 (Matthew 21: 23-27; Luke 20: 1-8)**

[27] They came again to Jerusalem, and as he was walking in the temple, the chief priests, and the scribes, and the elders came to him, [28] and they began saying to him, "By what authority do you do these things? Or who gave you this authority to do these things?" [29] Jesus said to them, *"I will ask you one question. Answer me, and I will tell you by what authority I do these things. [30] The baptism of John—was it from heaven, or from men? Answer me."* [31] They reasoned with themselves, saying, "If we should say, 'From heaven;' he will say, 'Why then did you not believe him?' [32] If we should say, 'From men'"—they feared the people, for all held John to really be a prophet. [33] They answered Jesus, "We don't know." Jesus said to them, *"Neither do I tell you by what authority I do these things."*

The Two Sons
- **Matthew 21: 28-32**

[28] *But what do you think? A man had two sons, and he came to the first, and said, 'Son, go work today in my vineyard.' [29] He answered, 'I will not,' but afterward he changed his mind, and went. [30] He came to the second, and said the same thing. He answered, 'I go, sir,' but he didn't go. [31] Which of the two did the will of his father?"* They said to him, "The first." Jesus said to them, *"Most certainly I tell you that the tax collectors and the prostitutes are entering into the Kingdom of God before you. [32] For John came to you in the way of righteousness, and you didn't believe him, but the tax collectors and the prostitutes believed him. When you saw it, you didn't even repent afterward, that you might believe him.*

The Tenants
- **Matthew 21: 33-46 (Mark 12: 1-12; Luke 20: 9-19)**

[33] *"Hear another parable. There was a man who was a master of a household, who planted a vineyard, set a hedge about it, dug a winepress in it, built a tower, leased it out to farmers, and went into another country. [34] When the season for the fruit drew near, he sent his servants to the farmers, to receive his fruit. [35] The farmers took his servants, beat one, killed another, and stoned another. [36]*

Again, he sent other servants more than the first: and they treated them the same way. [37] *But afterward he sent to them his son, saying, 'They will respect my son.'* [38] *But the farmers, when they saw the son, said among themselves, 'This is the heir. Come, let's kill him, and seize his inheritance.'* [39] *So they took him, and threw him out of the vineyard, and killed him.* [40] *When therefore the lord of the vineyard comes, what will he do to those farmers?"* [41] They told him, "He will miserably destroy those miserable men, and will leas out the vineyard to other farmers, who will give him the fruit in its season." [42] Jesus said to them, *"Did you never read in the Scriptures, 'The stone which the builders rejected, the same was made the head of the corner. This was from the Lord. It is marvelous in our eyes?'* [43] *"Therefore I tell you, the Kingdom of God will be taken away from you, and will be given to a nation bringing forth its fruit.* [44] *He who falls on this stone will be broken to pieces, but on whomever it will fall, it will scatter him as dust."* [45] When the chief priests and the Pharisees heard his parables, they perceived that he spoke about them. [46] When they sought to seize him, they feared the multitudes, because they considered him to be a prophet.

The Wedding Feast
- **Matthew 22: 1-14**

[1] Jesus answered and spoke again in parables to them, saying, [2] *"The Kingdom of Heaven is like a certain king, who made a marriage feast for his son,* [3] *and sent out his servants to call those who were invited to the marriage feast, but they would not come.* [4] *Again he sent out other servants, saying, 'Tell those who are invited, "Behold, I have prepared my dinner. My cattle and my fatlings are killed, and all things are ready. Come to the marriage feast!"'* [5] *But they made light of it, and went their ways, one to his own farm, another to his merchandise,* [6] *and the rest grabbed his servants, and treated them shamefully, and killed them.* [7] *When the king heard that, he was angry, and sent his armies, destroyed those murderers, and burned their city.* [8] *"Then he said to his servants, 'The wedding is ready, but those who were invited weren't worthy.* [9] *Go therefore to the inter-sections of the highways, and as many as you may find, invite to the marriage feast.'* [10] *Those servants went out into the highways, and*

gathered together as many as they found, both bad and good. The wedding was filled with guests. ¹¹ *But when the king came in to see the guests, he saw there a man who didn't have on wedding clothing,* ¹² *and he said to him, 'Friend, how did you come in here not wearing wedding clothing?' He was speechless.* ¹³ *Then the king said to the servants, 'Bind him hand and foot, take him away, and throw him into the outer darkness; there is where the weeping and grinding of teeth will be.'* ¹⁴ *For many are called, but few chosen."*

Paying Taxes to Caesar
- ### Luke 20: 20-26 (Matthew 22: 15-22; Mark 12: 13-17)

²⁰ They watched him, and sent out spies, who pretended to be righteous, that they might trap him in something he said, so as to deliver him up to the power and authority of the governor. ²¹ They asked him, "Teacher, we know that you say and teach what is right, and aren't partial to anyone, but truly teach the way of God. ²² Is it lawful for us to pay taxes to Caesar, or not?" ²³ But he perceived their craftiness, and said to them, *"Why do you test me?* ²⁴ *Show me a denarius. Whose image and inscription are on it?"* They answered, "Caesar's." ²⁵ He said to them, *"Then give to Caesar the things that are Caesar's, and to God the things that are God's."* ²⁶ They weren't able to trap him in his words before the people. They marveled at his answer, and were silent.

The Resurrection and Marriage
- ### Luke 20: 27-40 (Matthew 22: 23-33; Mark 12: 18-27)

²⁷ Some of the Sadducees came to him, those who deny that there is a resurrection. ²⁸ They asked him, "Teacher, Moses wrote to us that if a man's brother dies having a wife, and he is childless, his brother should take the wife, and raise up children for his brother. ²⁹ There were therefore seven brothers. The first took a wife, and died childless. ³⁰ The second took her as wife, and he died childless. ³¹ The third took her, and likewise the seven all left no children, and died. ³² Afterward the woman also died. ³³ Therefore in the resurrection whose wife of them will she be? For the seven had her as a wife." ³⁴ Jesus said to them, *"The children of this age marry, and are given in marriage.* ³⁵ *But those who are considered worthy to attain to that*

age and the resurrection from the dead, neither marry, nor are given in marriage. [36] For they can't die any more, for they are like the angels, and are children of God, being children of the resurrection. [37] But that the dead are raised, even Moses showed at the bush, when he called the Lord 'The God of Abraham, the God of Isaac, and the God of Jacob.' [38] Now he is not the God of the dead, but of the living, for all are alive to him." [39] Some of the scribes answered, "Teacher, you speak well." [40] They didn't dare to ask him any more questions.

The Greatest Commandments
• Mark 12: 28-34 (Matthew 22: 34-40)

[28] One of the scribes came, and heard them questioning together. Knowing that he had answered them well, asked him, "Which commandment is the greatest of all?" [29] Jesus answered, *"The greatest is, 'Hear, Israel, the Lord our God, the Lord is one: [30] you shall love the Lord your God with all your heart, and with all your soul, and with all your mind, and with all your strength.' This is the first commandment. [31] The second is like this, 'You shall love your neighbor as yourself.' There is no other commandment greater than these."* [32] The scribe said to him, "Truly, teacher, you have said well that he is one, and there is none other but he, [33] and to love him with all the heart, and with all the understanding, with all the soul, and with all the strength, and to love his neighbor as himself, is more important than all whole burnt offerings and sacrifices." [34] When Jesus saw that he answered wisely, he said to him, *"You are not far from the Kingdom of God."*

Whose Son is the Messiah?
• Matthew 22: 41-46 (Mark 12: 35-37; Luke 20: 41-44)

[41] Now while the Pharisees were gathered together, Jesus asked them a question, [42] saying, *"What do you think of the Christ? Whose son is he?"* They said to him, "Of David." [43] He said to them, *"How then does David in the Spirit call him Lord, saying, [44] 'The Lord said to my Lord, sit on my right hand, until I make your enemies a footstool for your feet?' [45] "If then David calls him Lord, how is he his son?"* [46] No one was able to answer him a word, neither did any man dare ask him any more questions from that day forth.

122

Warnings Against Hypocrisy
- **Matthew 23: 1-12 (Mark 12: 38-40; Luke 20: 45-47)**

[1] Then Jesus spoke to the multitudes and to his disciples, [2] saying, *"The scribes and the Pharisees sat on Moses' seat. [3] All things therefore whatever they tell you to observe, observe and do, but don't do their works; for they say, and don't do. [4] For they bind heavy burdens that are grievous to be borne, and lay them on men's shoulders; but they themselves will not lift a finger to help them. [5] But all their works they do to be seen by men. They make their phylacteries broad, enlarge the fringes of their garments, [6] and love the place of honor at feasts, the best seats in the synagogues, [7] the salutations in the marketplaces, and to be called 'Rabbi, Rabbi' by men. [8] But don't you be called 'Rabbi,' for one is your teacher, the Christ, and all of you are brothers. [9] Call no man on the earth your father, for one is your Father, he who is in heaven. [10] Neither be called masters, for one is your master, the Christ. [11] But he who is greatest among you will be your servant. [12] Whoever exalts himself will be humbled, and whoever humbles himself will be exalted.*

Seven Woes
- **Matthew 23: 13-36**

[13] *"Woe to you, scribes and Pharisees, hypocrites! For you devour widows' houses, and as a pretense you make long prayers. Therefore you will receive greater condemnation. [14] "But woe to you, scribes and Pharisees, hypocrites! Because you shut up the Kingdom of Heaven against men; for you don't enter in yourselves, neither do you allow those who are entering in to enter. [15] Woe to you, scribes and Pharisees, hypocrites! For you travel around by sea and land to make one proselyte; and when he becomes one, you make him twice as much of a son of Gehenna as yourselves. [16] "Woe to you, you blind guides, who say, 'Whoever swears by the temple, it is nothing; but whoever swears by the gold of the temple, he is obligated.'*

Jesus Grieves Over Jerusalem
- **Luke 13: 31-35 (Matthew 23: 37-39)**

[31] On that same day, some Pharisees came, saying to him, "Get out of here, and go away, for Herod wants to kill you." [32] He said to

them, *"Go and tell that fox, 'Behold, I cast out demons and perform cures today and tomorrow, and the third day I complete my mission. ³³ Nevertheless I must go on my way today and tomorrow and the next day, for it can't be that a prophet perish outside of Jerusalem.' ³⁴ "Jerusalem, Jerusalem, that kills the prophets, and stones those who are sent to her! How often I wanted to gather your children together, like a hen gathers her own brood under her wings, and you refused! ³⁵ Behold, your house is left to you desolate. I tell you, you will not see me, until you say, 'Blessed is he who comes in the name of the Lord!'"*

The Widow's Offering
- **Mark 12: 41-44 (Luke 21: 1-4)**

⁴¹ Jesus sat down opposite the treasury, and saw how the multitude cast money into the treasury. Many who were rich cast in much. ⁴² A poor widow came, and she cast in two small brass coins, which equal a quadrans coin. ⁴³ He called his disciples to himself, and said to them, *"Most certainly I tell you, this poor widow gave more than all those who are giving into the treasury, ⁴⁴ for they all gave out of their abundance, but she, out of her poverty, gave all that she had to live on."*

Jesus Teaches His Disciples
- **Matthew 24: 1-35 (Mark 13: 1-31; Luke 21: 5-33)**

¹ *Jesus went out from the temple, and was going on his way. His disciples came to him to show him the buildings of the temple. ² But he answered them, "You see all of these things, don't you? Most certainly I tell you, there will not be left here one stone on another, that will not be thrown down."* ³ As he sat on the Mount of Olives, the disciples came to him privately, saying, "Tell us, when will these things be? What is the sign of your coming, and of the end of the age?" ⁴ Jesus answered them, *"Be careful that no one leads you astray. ⁵ For many will come in my name, saying, 'I am the Christ,' and will lead many astray. ⁶ You will hear of wars and rumors of wars. See that you aren't troubled, for all this must happen, but the end is not yet. ⁷ For nation will rise against nation, and kingdom against kingdom; and there will be famines, plagues, and earthquakes in various places. ⁸*

But all these things are the beginning of birth pains. ⁹ Then they will deliver you up to oppression, and will kill you. You will be hated by all of the nations for my name's sake. ¹⁰ Then many will stumble, and will deliver up one another, and will hate one another. ¹¹ Many false prophets will arise, and will lead many astray. ¹² Because iniquity will be multiplied, the love of many will grow cold. ¹³ But he who endures to the end, the same will be saved. ¹⁴ This Good News of the Kingdom will be preached in the whole world for a testimony to all the nations, and then the end will come. ¹⁵ "When, therefore, you see the abomination of desolation, which was spoken of through Daniel the prophet, standing in the holy place (let the reader understand), ¹⁶ then let those who are in Judea flee to the mountains. ¹⁷ Let him who is on the housetop not go down to take out things that are in his house. ¹⁸ Let him who is in the field not return back to get his clothes. ¹⁹ But woe to those who are with child and to nursing mothers in those days! ²⁰ Pray that your flight will not be in the winter, nor on a Sabbath, ²¹ for then there will be great oppression, such as has not been from the beginning of the world until now, no, nor ever will be. ²² Unless those days had been shortened, no flesh would have been saved. But for the sake of the chosen ones, those days will be shortened. ²³ "Then if any man tells you, 'Behold, here is the Christ,' or, 'There,' don't believe it. ²⁴ For there will arise false christs, and false prophets, and they will show great signs and wonders, so as to lead astray, if possible, even the chosen ones. ²⁵ "Behold, I have told you beforehand. ²⁶ If therefore they tell you, 'Behold, he is in the wilderness,' don't go out; 'Behold, he is in the inner rooms,' don't believe it. ²⁷ For as the lightning flashes from the east, and is seen even to the west, so will be the coming of the Son of Man. ²⁸ For wherever the carcass is, there is where the vultures gather together. ²⁹ But immediately after the oppression of those days, the sun will be darkened, the moon will not give its light, the stars will fall from the sky, and the powers of the heavens will be shaken; ³⁰ and then the sign of the Son of Man will appear in the sky. Then all the tribes of the earth will mourn, and they will see the Son of Man coming on the clouds of the sky with power and great glory. ³¹ He will send out his angels with a great sound of a trumpet, and they will gather together his chosen ones from the four winds, from one end of the sky to the other. [32] *"Now from the fig tree learn this parable. When its branch has now become tender, and puts forth its leaves, you know that the summer is near.* [33] *Even so you also, when you see all these things, know that it is near, even at the doors.* [34] *Most certainly I tell you, this generation will not pass away, until all these things are accomplished.* [35] *Heaven and earth will pass away, but my words will not pass away.*

Signs of the End Times
• **Matthew 24: 36-51 (Mark 13: 32-37; Luke 21: 34-38)**

[36] *But no one knows of that day and hour, not even the angels of heaven, but my Father only.* [37] *"As the days of Noah were, so will be the coming of the Son of Man.* [38] *For as in those days which were before the flood they were eating and drinking, marrying and giving in marriage, until the day that Noah entered into the ship,* [39] *and they didn't know until the flood came, and took them all away, so will be the coming of the Son of Man.* [40] *Then two men will be in the field: one will be taken and one will be left;* [41] *two women grinding at the mill, one will be taken and one will be left.* [42] *Watch therefore, for you don't know in what hour your Lord comes.* [43] *But know this, that if the master of the house had known in what watch of the night the thief was coming, he would have watched, and would not have allowed his house to be broken into.* [44] *Therefore also be ready, for in an hour that you don't expect, the Son of Man will come.* [45] *"Who then is the faithful and wise servant, whom his lord has set over his household, to give them their food in due season?* [46] *Blessed is that servant whom his lord finds doing so when he comes.* [47] *Most certainly I tell you that he will set him over all that he has.* [48] *But if that evil servant should say in his heart, 'My lord is delaying his coming,'* [49] *and begins to beat his fellow servants, and eat and drink with the drunkards,* [50] *the lord of that servant will come in a day when he doesn't expect it, and in an hour when he doesn't know it,* [51] *and will cut him in pieces, and appoint his portion with the hypocrites. There is where the weeping and grinding of teeth will be.*

The Ten Virgins
  • **Matthew 25: 1-13**

¹ "Then the Kingdom of Heaven will be like ten virgins, who took their lamps, and went out to meet the bridegroom. ² Five of them were foolish, and five were wise. ³ Those who were foolish, when they took their lamps, took no oil with them, ⁴ but the wise took oil in their vessels with their lamps. ⁵ Now while the bridegroom delayed, they all slumbered and slept. ⁶ But at midnight there was a cry, 'Behold! The bridegroom is coming! Come out to meet him!' ⁷ Then all those virgins arose, and trimmed their lamps. ⁸ The foolish said to the wise, 'Give us some of your oil, for our lamps are going out.' ⁹ But the wise answered, saying, 'What if there isn't enough for us and you? You go rather to those who sell, and buy for yourselves.' ¹⁰ While they went away to buy, the bridegroom came, and those who were ready went in with him to the marriage feast, and the door was shut. ¹¹ Afterward the other virgins also came, saying, 'Lord, Lord, open to us.' ¹² But he answered, 'Most certainly I tell you, I don't know you.' ¹³ Watch therefore, for you don't know the day nor the hour in which the Son of Man is coming.

The Talents
  • **Matthew 25: 14-30**

¹⁴ "For it is like a man, going into another country, who called his own servants, and entrusted his goods to them. ¹⁵ To one he gave five talents, to another two, to another one; to each according to his own ability. Then he went on his journey. ¹⁶ Immediately he who received the five talents went and traded with them, and made another five talents. ¹⁷ In the same way, he also who got the two gained another two. ¹⁸ But he who received the one went away and dug in the earth, and hid his lord's money. ¹⁹ "Now after a long time the lord of those servants came, and reconciled accounts with them. ²⁰ He who received the five talents came and brought another five talents, saying, 'Lord, you delivered to me five talents. Behold, I have gained another five talents besides them.' ²¹ "His lord said to him, 'Well done, good and faithful servant. You have been faithful over a few things, I will set you over many things. Enter into the joy of your lord.' ²² "He also who got the two talents came and said, 'Lord, you delivered to me two talents. Behold, I have gained another two talents besides them.' ²³ "His lord said to him, 'Well done, good and faithful servant. You have been faithful over a few things, I will set you over many things. Enter into the joy of your lord.' ²⁴ "He also who had received the one talent came and said, 'Lord, I knew you that you are a hard man, reaping where you did not sow, and gathering where you did not scatter. ²⁵ I was afraid, and went away and hid your talent in the earth. Behold, you have what is yours.' ²⁶ "But his lord answered him, 'You wicked and slothful servant. You knew that I reap where I didn't sow, and gather where I didn't scatter. ²⁷ You ought therefore to have deposited my money with the bankers, and at my coming I should have received back my own with interest. ²⁸ Take away therefore the talent from him, and give it to him who has the ten talents. ²⁹ For to everyone who has will be given, and he will have abundance, but from him who doesn't have, even that which he has will be taken away. ³⁰ Throw out the unprofitable servant into the outer darkness, where there will be weeping and gnashing of teeth.'

The Sheep and the Goats
- **Matthew 25: 31-46**

³¹ "But when the Son of Man comes in his glory, and all the holy angels with him, then he will sit on the throne of his glory. ³² Before him all the nations will be gathered, and he will separate them one from another, as a shepherd separates the sheep from the goats. ³³ He will set the sheep on his right hand, but the goats on the left. ³⁴ Then the King will tell those on his right hand, 'Come, blessed of my Father, inherit the Kingdom prepared for you from the foundation of the world; ³⁵ for I was hungry, and you gave me food to eat. I was thirsty, and you gave me drink. I was a stranger, and you took me in. ³⁶ I was naked, and you clothed me. I was sick, and you visited me. I was in prison, and you came to me.' ³⁷ "Then the righteous will answer him, saying, 'Lord, when did we see you hungry, and feed you; or thirsty, and give you a drink? ³⁸ When did we see you as a stranger, and take you in; or naked, and clothe you? ³⁹ When did we see you sick, or in prison, and come to you?' ⁴⁰ "The King will answer them, 'Most certainly I tell you, inasmuch as you did it to one of the least of these my brothers, you did it to me.' ⁴¹ Then he

will say also to those on the left hand, 'Depart from me, you cursed, into the eternal fire which is prepared for the devil and his angels; ⁴² *for I was hungry, and you didn't give me food to eat; I was thirsty, and you gave me no drink;* ⁴³ *I was a stranger, and you didn't take me in; naked, and you didn't clothe me; sick, and in prison, and you didn't visit me.'* ⁴⁴ *"Then they will also answer, saying, 'Lord, when did we see you hungry, or thirsty, or a stranger, or naked, or sick, or in prison, and didn't help you?'* ⁴⁵ *"Then he will answer them, saying, 'Most certainly I tell you, inasmuch as you didn't do it to one of the least of these, you didn't do it to me.'* ⁴⁶ *These will go away into eternal punishment, but the righteous into eternal life."*

Preparation for the Passover
- **Luke 22: 7-13 (Matthew 26: 17-19; Mark 14: 12-16)**

⁷ The day of unleavened bread came, on which the Passover must be sacrificed. ⁸ He sent Peter and John, saying, *"Go and prepare the Passover for us, that we may eat."* ⁹ They said to him, "Where do you want us to prepare?" ¹⁰ He said to them, *"Behold, when you have entered into the city, a man carrying a pitcher of water will meet you. Follow him into the house which he enters.* ¹¹ *Tell the master of the house, 'The Teacher says to you, "Where is the guest room, where I may eat the Passover with my disciples?"'* ¹² *He will show you a large, furnished upper room. Make preparations there."* ¹³ They went, found things as he had told them, and they prepared the Passover.

The Last Supper
- **John 13: 1-17**

¹ Now before the feast of the Passover, Jesus, knowing that his time had come that he would depart from this world to the Father, having loved his own who were in the world, he loved them to the end. ² During supper, the devil having already put into the heart of Judas Iscariot, Simon's son, to betray him, ³ Jesus, knowing that the Father had given all things into his hands, and that he came forth from God, and was going to God, ⁴ arose from supper, and laid aside his outer garments. He took a towel, and wrapped a towel around his waist. ⁵ Then he poured water into the basin, and began to wash the disci-

ples' feet, and to wipe them with the towel that was wrapped around him. ⁶Then he came to Simon Peter. He said to him, "Lord, do you wash my feet?" ⁷Jesus answered him, *"You don't know what I am doing now, but you will understand later."* ⁸Peter said to him, "You will never wash my feet!" Jesus answered him, *"If I don't wash you, you have no part with me."* ⁹Simon Peter said to him, "Lord, not my feet only, but also my hands and my head!" ¹⁰Jesus said to him, *"Someone who has bathed only needs to have his feet washed, but is completely clean. You are clean, but not all of you."* ¹¹For he knew him who would betray him, therefore he said, *"You are not all clean."* ¹²So when he had washed their feet, put his outer garment back on, and sat down again, he said to them, *"Do you know what I have done to you? ¹³You call me, 'Teacher' and 'Lord.' You say so correctly, for so I am. ¹⁴If I then, the Lord and the Teacher, have washed your feet, you also ought to wash one another's feet. ¹⁵For I have given you an example, that you also should do as I have done to you. ¹⁶Most certainly I tell you, a servant is not greater than his lord, neither one who is sent greater than he who sent him. ¹⁷If you know these things, blessed are you if you do them.*

The First Communion
* ### Luke 22: 14-20 (Matthew 26: 26-30; Mark 14: 22-26)
¹⁴When the hour had come, he sat down with the twelve apostles. ¹⁵He said to them, *"I have earnestly desired to eat this Passover with you before I suffer, ¹⁶for I tell you, I will no longer by any means eat of it until it is fulfilled in the Kingdom of God."* ¹⁷He received a cup, and when he had given thanks, he said, *"Take this, and share it among yourselves, ¹⁸for I tell you, I will not drink at all again from the fruit of the vine, until the Kingdom of God comes."* ¹⁹He took bread, and when he had given thanks, he broke it, and gave to them, saying, *"This is my body which is given for you. Do this in memory of me."* ²⁰Likewise, he took the cup after supper, saying, *"This cup is the new covenant in my blood, which is poured out for you.*

Jesus Predicts His Betrayal
- **John 13: 18-30 (Matthew 26: 20-25; Mark 14: 17-21; Luke 22: 21-23)**

¹⁸ I don't speak concerning all of you. I know whom I have chosen. But that the Scripture may be fulfilled, 'He who eats bread with me has lifted up his heel against me.' ¹⁹ From now on, I tell you before it happens, that when it happens, you may believe that I am he. ²⁰ Most certainly I tell you, he who receives whomever I send, receives me; and he who receives me, receives him who sent me." ²¹ When Jesus had said this, he was troubled in spirit, and testified, *"Most certainly I tell you that one of you will betray me."* ²² The disciples looked at one another, perplexed about whom he spoke. ²³ One of his disciples, whom Jesus loved, was at the table, leaning against Jesus' breast. ²⁴ Simon Peter therefore beckoned to him, and said to him, "Tell us who it is of whom he speaks." ²⁵ He, leaning back, as he was, on Jesus' breast, asked him, "Lord, who is it?" ²⁶ Jesus therefore answered, *"It is he to whom I will give this piece of bread when I have dipped it."* So when he had dipped the piece of bread, he gave it to Judas, the son of Simon Iscariot. ²⁷ After the piece of bread, then Satan entered into him. Then Jesus said to him, *"What you do, do quickly."* ²⁸ Now no man at the table knew why he said this to him. ²⁹ For some thought, because Judas had the money box, that Jesus said to him, "Buy what things we need for the feast," or that he should give something to the poor. ³⁰ Therefore having received that morsel, he went out immediately. It was night.

True Greatness
- **Luke 22: 24-30**

²⁴ There arose also a contention among them, which of them was considered to be greatest. ²⁵ He said to them, *"The kings of the nations lord it over them, and those who have authority over them are called 'benefactors.' ²⁶ But not so with you. But one who is the greater among you, let him become as the younger, and one who is governing, as one who serves. ²⁷ For who is greater, one who sits at the table, or one who serves? Isn't it he who sits at the table? But I am in your midst as one who serves. ²⁸ But you are those who have continued with me in my trials. ²⁹ I confer on you a kingdom, even as*

my Father conferred on me, *[30] that you may eat and drink at my table in my Kingdom. You will sit on thrones, judging the twelve tribes of Israel."*

Jesus Predicts Peter's Denial
- **John 13: 31-38 (Matthew 26: 31-35; Mark 14: 27-31; Luke 22: 31-34)**

[31] When he had gone out, Jesus said, *"Now the Son of Man has been glorified, and God has been glorified in him. [32] If God has been glorified in him, God will also glorify him in himself, and he will glorify him immediately. [33] Little children, I will be with you a little while longer. You will seek me, and as I said to the Jews, 'Where I am going, you can't come,' so now I tell you. [34] A new commandment I give to you, that you love one another, just like I have loved you; that you also love one another. [35] By this everyone will know that you are my disciples, if you have love for one another."* [36] Simon Peter said to him, "Lord, where are you going?" Jesus answered, *"Where I am going, you can't follow now, but you will follow afterwards."* [37] Peter said to him, "Lord, why can't I follow you now? I will lay down my life for you." [38] Jesus answered him, *"Will you lay down your life for me? Most certainly I tell you, the rooster won't crow until you have denied me three times.*

Jesus' Instructions to His Disciples
- **Luke 22: 35-38**

[35] He said to them, *"When I sent you out without purse, and wallet, and shoes, did you lack anything?"* They said, "Nothing." [36] Then he said to them, *"But now, whoever has a purse, let him take it, and likewise a wallet. Whoever has none, let him sell his cloak, and buy a sword. [37] For I tell you that this which is written must still be fulfilled in me: 'He was counted with transgressors.' For that which concerns me has an end."* [38] They said, "Lord, behold, here are two swords." He said to them, *"That is enough."*

Jesus Comforts His Disciples
- ### John 14: 1-4

¹ "Don't let your heart be troubled. Believe in God. Believe also in me. ² In my Father's house are many homes. If it weren't so, I would have told you. I am going to prepare a place for you. ³ If I go and prepare a place for you, I will come again, and will receive you to myself; that where I am, you may be there also. ⁴ Where I go, you know, and you know the way."

The Way, the Truth, and the Life
- ### John 14: 5-14

⁵ Thomas said to him, "Lord, we don't know where you are going. How can we know the way?" ⁶ Jesus said to him, *"I am the way, the truth, and the life. No one comes to the Father, except through me. ⁷ If you had known me, you would have known my Father also. From now on, you know him, and have seen him."* ⁸ Philip said to him, "Lord, show us the Father, and that will be enough for us." ⁹ Jesus said to him, *"Have I been with you such a long time, and do you not know me, Philip? He who has seen me has seen the Father. How do you say, 'Show us the Father?' ¹⁰ Don't you believe that I am in the Father, and the Father in me? The words that I tell you, I speak not from myself; but the Father who lives in me does his works. ¹¹ Believe me that I am in the Father, and the Father in me; or else believe me for the very works' sake. ¹² Most certainly I tell you, he who believes in me, the works that I do, he will do also; and he will do greater works than these, because I am going to my Father. ¹³ Whatever you will ask in my name, that will I do, that the Father may be glorified in the Son. ¹⁴ If you will ask anything in my name, I will do it.*

Promise of the Holy Spirit
- ### John 14: 15-31

¹⁵ If you love me, keep my commandments. ¹⁶ I will pray to the Father, and he will give you another Counselor, that he may be with you forever,— ¹⁷ the Spirit of truth, whom the world can't receive; for it doesn't see him, neither knows him. You know him, for he lives with you, and will be in you. ¹⁸ I will not leave you orphans. I will come to you. ¹⁹ Yet a little while, and the world will see me no more; but you will see me. Because I live, you will live also. [20] *In that day you will know that I am in my Father, and you in me, and I in you.* [21] *One who has my commandments, and keeps them, that person is one who loves me. One who loves me will be loved by my Father, and I will love him, and will reveal myself to him."* [22] Judas (not Iscariot) said to him, "Lord, what has happened that you are about to reveal yourself to us, and not to the world?" [23] Jesus answered him, *"If a man loves me, he will keep my word. My Father will love him, and we will come to him, and make our home with him.* [24] *He who doesn't love me doesn't keep my words. The word which you hear isn't mine, but the Father's who sent me.* [25] *I have said these things to you, while still living with you.* [26] *But the Counselor, the Holy Spirit, whom the Father will send in my name, he will teach you all things, and will remind you of all that I said to you.* [27] *Peace I leave with you. My peace I give to you; not as the world gives, give I to you. Don't let your heart be troubled, neither let it be fearful.* [28] *You heard how I told you, 'I go away, and I come to you.' If you loved me, you would have rejoiced, because I said 'I am going to my Father;' for the Father is greater than I.* [29] *Now I have told you before it happens so that, when it happens, you may believe.* [30] *I will no more speak much with you, for the prince of the world comes, and he has nothing in me.* [31] *But that the world may know that I love the Father, and as the Father commanded me, even so I do. Arise, let us go from here.*

The Vine and its Branches
• John 15: 1-17

[1] *"I am the true vine, and my Father is the farmer.* [2] *Every branch in me that doesn't bear fruit, he takes away. Every branch that bears fruit, he prunes, that it may bear more fruit.* [3] *You are already pruned clean because of the word which I have spoken to you.* [4] *Remain in me, and I in you. As the branch can't bear fruit by itself, unless it remains in the vine, so neither can you, unless you remain in me.* [5] *I am the vine. You are the branches. He who remains in me, and I in him, the same bears much fruit, for apart from me you can do nothing.* [6] *If a man doesn't remain in me, he is thrown out as a branch, and is withered; and they gather them, throw them into the fire, and they are burned.* [7] *If you remain in me, and my words*

remain in you, you will ask whatever you desire, and it will be done for you. [8] "In this is my Father glorified, that you bear much fruit; and so you will be my disciples. [9] Even as the Father has loved me, I also have loved you. Remain in my love. [10] If you keep my commandments, you will remain in my love; even as I have kept my Father's commandments, and remain in his love. [11] I have spoken these things to you, that my joy may remain in you, and that your joy may be made full. [12] "This is my commandment, that you love one another, even as I have loved you. [13] Greater love has no one than this, that someone lay down his life for his friends. [14] You are my friends, if you do whatever I command you. [15] No longer do I call you servants, for the servant doesn't know what his lord does. But I have called you friends, for everything that I heard from my Father, I have made known to you. [16] You didn't choose me, but I chose you, and appointed you, that you should go and bear fruit, and that your fruit should remain; that whatever you will ask of the Father in my name, he may give it to you. [17] "I command these things to you, that you may love one another.*

The World Hates the Disciples
- **John 15: 18-27 & 16: 1-4**

[18] If the world hates you, you know that it has hated me before it hated you. [19] If you were of the world, the world would love its own. But because you are not of the world, since I chose you out of the world, therefore the world hates you. [20] Remember the word that I said to you: 'A servant is not greater than his lord.' If they persecuted me, they will also persecute you. If they kept my word, they will keep yours also. [21] But all these things will they do to you for my name's sake, because they don't know him who sent me. [22] If I had not come and spoken to them, they would not have had sin; but now they have no excuse for their sin. [23] He who hates me, hates my Father also. [24] If I hadn't done among them the works which no one else did, they wouldn't have had sin. But now have they seen and also hated both me and my Father. [25] But this happened so that the word may be fulfilled which was written in their law, 'They hated me without a cause.' [26] "When the Counselor has come, whom I will send to you from the Father, the Spirit of truth, who proceeds from the Father, he*

will testify about me. [27] *You will also testify, because you have been with me from the beginning.*

[1] "These things have I spoken to you, so that you wouldn't be caused to stumble. [2] They will put you out of the synagogues. Yes, the time comes that whoever kills you will think that he offers service to God. [3] They will do these things because they have not known the Father, nor me. [4] But I have told you these things, so that when the time comes, you may remember that I told you about them. I didn't tell you these things from the beginning, because I was with you.

Work of the Holy Spirit
* **John 16: 5-16**

[5] *But now I am going to him who sent me, and none of you asks me, 'Where are you going?'* [6] *But because I have told you these things, sorrow has filled your heart.* [7] *Nevertheless I tell you the truth: It is to your advantage that I go away, for if I don't go away, the Counselor won't come to you. But if I go, I will send him to you.* [8] *When he has come, he will convict the world about sin, about righteousness, and about judgment;* [9] *about sin, because they don't believe in me;* [10] *about righteousness, because I am going to my Father, and you won't see me anymore;* [11] *about judgment, because the prince of this world has been judged.* [12] *"I have yet many things to tell you, but you can't bear them now.* [13] *However when he, the Spirit of truth, has come, he will guide you into all truth, for he will not speak from himself; but whatever he hears, he will speak. He will declare to you things that are coming.* [14] *He will glorify me, for he will take from what is mine, and will declare it to you.* [15] *All things whatever the Father has are mine; therefore I said that he takes of mine, and will declare it to you.* [16] *A little while, and you will not see me. Again a little while, and you will see me."*

The Disciples Grief Will Change to Joy
* **John 16: 17-33**

[17] Some of his disciples therefore said to one another, "What is this that he says to us, *'A little while, and you won't see me, and again a little while, and you will see me;'* and, *'Because I go to the Father?'*

" ¹⁸ They said therefore, "What is this that he says, *'A little while?'* We don't know what he is saying." ¹⁹ Therefore Jesus perceived that they wanted to ask him, and he said to them, *"Do you inquire among yourselves concerning this, that I said, 'A little while, and you won't see me, and again a little while, and you will see me?' ²⁰ Most certainly I tell you, that you will weep and lament, but the world will rejoice. You will be sorrowful, but your sorrow will be turned into joy. ²¹ A woman, when she gives birth, has sorrow, because her time has come. But when she has delivered the child, she doesn't remember the anguish any more, for the joy that a human being is born into the world. ²² Therefore you now have sorrow, but I will see you again, and your heart will rejoice, and no one will take your joy away from you. ²³ "In that day you will ask me no questions. Most certainly I tell you, whatever you may ask of the Father in my name, he will give it to you. ²⁴ Until now, you have asked nothing in my name. Ask, and you will receive, that your joy may be made full. ²⁵ I have spoken these things to you in figures of speech. But the time is coming when I will no more speak to you in figures of speech, but will tell you plainly about the Father. ²⁶ In that day you will ask in my name; and I don't say to you, that I will pray to the Father for you, ²⁷ for the Father himself loves you, because you have loved me, and have believed that I came forth from God. ²⁸ I came out from the Father, and have come into the world. Again, I leave the world, and go to the Father."* ²⁹ His disciples said to him, "Behold, now you speak plainly, and speak no figures of speech. ³⁰ Now we know that you know all things, and don't need for anyone to question you. By this we believe that you came forth from God." ³¹ Jesus answered them, *"Do you now believe? ³² Behold, the time is coming, yes, and has now come, that you will be scattered, everyone to his own place, and you will leave me alone. Yet I am not alone, because the Father is with me. ³³ I have told you these things, that in me you may have peace. In the world you have oppression; but cheer up! I have overcome the world."*

Jesus Prays for Himself
- ## John 17: 1-5

[1] Jesus said these things, and lifting up his eyes to heaven, he said, *"Father, the time has come. Glorify your Son, that your Son may also glorify you;* [2] *even as you gave him authority over all flesh, he will give eternal life to all whom you have given him.* [3] *This is eternal life, that they should know you, the only true God, and him whom you sent, Jesus Christ.* [4] *I glorified you on the earth. I have accomplished the work which you have given me to do.* [5] *Now, Father, glorify me with your own self with the glory which I had with you before the world existed.*

Jesus Prays for His Disciples
- ## John 17: 6-19

[6] *I revealed your name to the people whom you have given me out of the world. They were yours, and you have given them to me. They have kept your word.* [7] *Now they have known that all things whatever you have given me are from you,* [8] *for the words which you have given me I have given to them, and they received them, and knew for sure that I came forth from you, and they have believed that you sent me.* [9] *I pray for them. I don't pray for the world, but for those whom you have given me, for they are yours.* [10] *All things that are mine are yours, and yours are mine, and I am glorified in them.* [11] *I am no more in the world, but these are in the world, and I am coming to you. Holy Father, keep them through your name which you have given me, that they may be one, even as we are.* [12] *While I was with them in the world, I kept them in your name. Those whom you have given me I have kept. None of them is lost, except the son of destruction, that the Scripture might be fulfilled.* [13] *But now I come to you, and I say these things in the world, that they may have my joy made full in themselves.* [14] *I have given them your word. The world hated them, because they are not of the world, even as I am not of the world.* [15] *I pray not that you would take them from the world, but that you would keep them from the evil one.* [16] *They are not of the world even as I am not of the world.* [17] *Sanctify them in your truth. Your word is truth.* [18] *As you sent me into the world, even so I have sent*

them into the world. [19] For their sakes I sanctify myself, that they themselves also may be sanctified in truth.

Jesus Prays for All Believers
- ## John 17: 20-26

[20] Not for these only do I pray, but for those also who believe in me through their word, [21] that they may all be one; even as you, Father, are in me, and I in you, that they also may be one in us; that the world may believe that you sent me. [22] The glory which you have given me, I have given to them; that they may be one, even as we are one; [23] I in them, and you in me, that they may be perfected into one; that the world may know that you sent me, and loved them, even as you loved me. [24] Father, I desire that they also whom you have given me be with me where I am, that they may see my glory, which you have given me, for you loved me before the foundation of the world. [25] Righteous Father, the world hasn't known you, but I knew you; and these knew that you sent me. [26] I made known to them your name, and will make it known; that the love with which you loved me may be in them, and I in them."

The Mount of Olives
- ## Matthew 26: 36-46 (Mark 14: 32-42; Luke 22: 39-46)

[36] Then Jesus came with them to a place called Gethsemane, and said to his disciples, *"Sit here, while I go there and pray."* [37] He took with him Peter and the two sons of Zebedee, and began to be sorrowful and severely troubled. [38] Then he said to them, *"My soul is exceedingly sorrowful, even to death. Stay here, and watch with me."* [39] He went forward a little, fell on his face, and prayed, saying, *"My Father, if it is possible, let this cup pass away from me; nevertheless, not what I desire, but what you desire."* [40] He came to the disciples, and found them sleeping, and said to Peter, *"What, couldn't you watch with me for one hour? [41] Watch and pray, that you don't enter into temptation. The spirit indeed is willing, but the flesh is weak."* [42] Again, a second time he went away, and prayed, saying, *"My Father, if this cup can't pass away from me unless I drink it, your desire be done."* [43] He came again and found them sleeping, for their eyes were heavy. [44] He left them again, went away, and prayed a third

time, saying the same words. [45] Then he came to his disciples, and said to them, *"Sleep on now, and take your rest. Behold, the hour is at hand, and the Son of Man is betrayed into the hands of sinners. [46] Arise, let's be going. Behold, he who betrays me is at hand."*

Jesus is Arrested
- ### Luke 22: 47-53 (Matthew 26: 47-56; Mark 14: 43-52; John 18: 1-14)

[47] While he was still speaking, behold, a multitude, and he who was called Judas, one of the twelve, was leading them. He came near to Jesus to kiss him. [48] But Jesus said to him, *"Judas, do you betray the Son of Man with a kiss?"* [49] When those who were around him saw what was about to happen, they said to him, "Lord, shall we strike with the sword?" [50] A certain one of them struck the servant of the high priest, and cut off his right ear. [51] But Jesus answered, *"Let me at least do this"* —and he touched his ear, and healed him. [52] Jesus said to the chief priests, captains of the temple, and elders, who had come against him, *"Have you come out as against a robber, with swords and clubs? [53] When I was with you in the temple daily, you didn't stretch out your hands against me. But this is your hour, and the power of darkness."*

Peter's First Denial of Jesus
- ### John 18: 15-17 (Matthew 26: 69-70; Mark 14: 66-68; Luke 22: 54-57)

[15] Simon Peter followed Jesus, as did another disciple. Now that disciple was known to the high priest, and entered in with Jesus into the court of the high priest; [16] but Peter was standing at the door outside. So the other disciple, who was known to the high priest, went out and spoke to her who kept the door, and brought in Peter. [17] Then the maid who kept the door said to Peter, "Are you also one of this man's disciples?" He said, "I am not."

Jesus Before the Council of Elders
- **Mark 14: 53-65 (Matthew 26: 57-68; Luke 22: 63-71; John 18: 18-24)**

[53] They led Jesus away to the high priest. All the chief priests, the elders, and the scribes came together with him. [54] Peter had followed him from a distance, until he came into the court of the high priest. He was sitting with the officers, and warming himself in the light of the fire. [55] Now the chief priests and the whole council sought witnesses against Jesus to put him to death, and found none. [56] For many gave false testimony against him, and their testimony didn't agree with each other. [57] Some stood up, and gave false testimony against him, saying, [58] "We heard him say, 'I will destroy this temple that is made with hands, and in three days I will build another made without hands.'" [59] Even so, their testimony did not agree. [60] The high priest stood up in the midst, and asked Jesus, "Have you no answer? What is it which these testify against you?" [61] But he stayed quiet, and answered nothing. Again the high priest asked him, "Are you the Christ, the Son of the Blessed?" [62] Jesus said, *"I am. You will see the Son of Man sitting at the right hand of Power, and coming with the clouds of the sky."* [63] The high priest tore his clothes, and said, "What further need have we of witnesses? [64] You have heard the blasphemy! What do you think?" They all condemned him to be worthy of death. [65] Some began to spit on him, and to cover his face, and to beat him with fists, and to tell him, "Prophesy!" The officers struck him with the palms of their hands.

Peter's Second and Third Denials
- **Luke 22: 58-62 (Matthew 26: 71-75; Mark 14: 69-72; John 18: 25-27)**

[58] After a little while someone else saw him, and said, "You also are one of them!" But Peter answered, "Man, I am not!" [59] After about one hour passed, another confidently affirmed, saying, "Truly this man also was with him, for he is a Galilean!" [60] But Peter said, "Man, I don't know what you are talking about!" Immediately, while he was still speaking, a rooster crowed. [61] The Lord turned, and looked at Peter. Then Peter remembered the Lord's word, how he said to

him, *"Before the rooster crows you will deny me three times."* [62] He went out, and wept bitterly.

The Religious Leaders Condemn Jesus
• **Matthew 27: 1-2 (Mark 15: 1)**

[1] Now when morning had come, all the chief priests and the elders of the people took counsel against Jesus to put him to death: [2] and they bound him, and led him away, and delivered him up to Pontius Pilate, the governor.

Judas Hangs Himself
• **Matthew 27: 3-10**

[3] Then Judas, who betrayed him, when he saw that Jesus was condemned, felt remorse, and brought back the thirty pieces of silver to the chief priests and elders, [4] saying, "I have sinned in that I betrayed innocent blood." But they said, "What is that to us? You see to it." [5] He threw down the pieces of silver in the sanctuary, and departed. He went away and hanged himself. [6] The chief priests took the pieces of silver, and said, "It's not lawful to put them into the treasury, since it is the price of blood." [7] They took counsel, and bought the potter's field with them, to bury strangers in. [8] Therefore that field was called "The Field of Blood" to this day. [9] Then that which was spoken through Jeremiah the prophet was fulfilled, saying, "They took the thirty pieces of silver, the price of him upon whom a price had been set, whom some of the children of Israel priced, [10] and they gave them for the potter's field, as the Lord commanded me."

Jesus Before Pilate and Herod
• **Luke 23: 1-25 (Matthew 27: 11-26; Mark 15: 2-15; John 18: 28-40)**

[1] The whole company of them rose up and brought him before Pilate. [2] They began to accuse him, saying, "We found this man perverting the nation, forbidding paying taxes to Caesar, and saying that he himself is Christ, a king." [3] Pilate asked him, "Are you the King of the Jews?" He answered him, *"So you say."* [4] Pilate said to the chief priests and the multitudes, "I find no basis for a charge against this man." [5] But they insisted, saying, "He stirs up the people, teaching

throughout all Judea, beginning from Galilee even to this place." [6] But when Pilate heard Galilee mentioned, he asked if the man was a Galilean. [7] When he found out that he was in Herod's jurisdiction, he sent him to Herod, who was also in Jerusalem during those days. [8] Now when Herod saw Jesus, he was exceedingly glad, for he had wanted to see him for a long time, because he had heard many things about him. He hoped to see some miracle done by him. [9] He questioned him with many words, but he gave no answers. [10] The chief priests and the scribes stood, vehemently accusing him. [11] Herod with his soldiers humiliated him and mocked him. Dressing him in luxurious clothing, they sent him back to Pilate. [12] Herod and Pilate became friends with each other that very day, for before that they were enemies with each other. [13] Pilate called together the chief priests and the rulers and the people, [14] and said to them, "You brought this man to me as one that perverts the people, and see, I have examined him before you, and found no basis for a charge against this man concerning those things of which you accuse him. [15] Neither has Herod, for I sent you to him, and see, nothing worthy of death has been done by him. [16] I will therefore chastise him and release him." [17] Now he had to release one prisoner to them at the feast. [18] But they all cried out together, saying, "Away with this man! Release to us Barabbas!" — [19] one who was thrown into prison for a certain revolt in the city, and for murder. [20] Then Pilate spoke to them again, wanting to release Jesus, [21] but they shouted, saying, "Crucify! Crucify him!" [22] He said to them the third time, "Why? What evil has this man done? I have found no capital crime in him. I will therefore chastise him and release him." [23] But they were urgent with loud voices, asking that he might be crucified. Their voices and the voices of the chief priests prevailed. [24] Pilate decreed that what they asked for should be done. [25] He released him who had been thrown into prison for insurrection and murder, for whom they asked, but he delivered Jesus up to their will.

The Soldiers Mock Jesus Again
• **Matthew 27: 27-30 (Mark 15: 16-20; John 19: 1-3)**
[27] Then the governor's soldiers took Jesus into the Praetorium, and gathered the whole garrison together against him. [28] They stripped

him, and put a scarlet robe on him. [29] They braided a crown of thorns and put it on his head, and a reed in his right hand; and they kneeled down before him, and mocked him, saying, "Hail, King of the Jews!" [30] They spat on him, and took the reed and struck him on the head.

Jesus is Sentenced to Death
   • **John 19: 4-16**

[4] Then Pilate went out again, and said to them, "Behold, I bring him out to you, that you may know that I find no basis for a charge against him." [5] Jesus therefore came out, wearing the crown of thorns and the purple garment. Pilate said to them, "Behold, the man!" [6] When therefore the chief priests and the officers saw him, they shouted, saying, "Crucify! Crucify!" Pilate said to them, "Take him yourselves, and crucify him, for I find no basis for a charge against him." [7] The Jews answered him, "We have a law, and by our law he ought to die, because he made himself the Son of God." [8] When therefore Pilate heard this saying, he was more afraid. [9] He entered into the Praetorium again, and said to Jesus, "Where are you from?" But Jesus gave him no answer. [10] Pilate therefore said to him, "Aren't you speaking to me? Don't you know that I have power to release you, and have power to crucify you?" [11] Jesus answered, *"You would have no power at all against me, unless it were given to you from above. Therefore he who delivered me to you has greater sin."* [12] At this, Pilate was seeking to release him, but the Jews cried out, saying, "If you release this man, you aren't Caesar's friend! Everyone who makes himself a king speaks against Caesar!" [13] When Pilate therefore heard these words, he brought Jesus out, and sat down on the judgment seat at a place called "The Pavement," but in Hebrew, "Gabbatha." [14] Now it was the Preparation Day of the Passover, at about the sixth hour. He said to the Jews, "Behold, your King!" [15] They cried out, "Away with him! Away with him! Crucify him!" Pilate said to them, "Shall I crucify your King?" The chief priests answered, "We have no king but Caesar!" [16] So then he delivered him to them to be crucified. So they took Jesus and led him away.

The Crucifixion of Jesus

- **Luke 23: 26-43 (Matthew 27: 31-44; Mark 15: 21-32; John 19: 17-27)**

[26] When they led him away, they grabbed one Simon of Cyrene, coming from the country, and laid on him the cross, to carry it after Jesus. [27] A great multitude of the people followed him, including women who also mourned and lamented him. [28] But Jesus, turning to them, said, *"Daughters of Jerusalem, don't weep for me, but weep for yourselves and for your children. [29] For behold, the days are coming in which they will say, 'Blessed are the barren, the wombs that never bore, and the breasts that never nursed.' [30] Then they will begin to tell the mountains, 'Fall on us!' and tell the hills, 'Cover us.' [31] For if they do these things in the green tree, what will be done in the dry?"* [32] There were also others, two criminals, led with him to be put to death. [33] When they came to the place that is called The Skull, they crucified him there with the criminals, one on the right and the other on the left. [34] Jesus said, *"Father, forgive them, for they don't know what they are doing."* Dividing his garments among them, they cast lots. [35] The people stood watching. The rulers with them also scoffed at him, saying, "He saved others. Let him save himself, if this is the Christ of God, his chosen one!" [36] The soldiers also mocked him, coming to him and offering him vinegar, [37] and saying, "If you are the King of the Jews, save yourself!" [38] An inscription was also written over him in letters of Greek, Latin, and Hebrew: "THIS IS THE KING OF THE JEWS." [39] One of the criminals who was hanged insulted him, saying, "If you are the Christ, save yourself and us!" [40] But the other answered, and rebuking him said, "Don't you even fear God, seeing you are under the same condemnation? [41] And we indeed justly, for we receive the due reward for our deeds, but this man has done nothing wrong." [42] He said to Jesus, "Lord, remember me when you come into your Kingdom." [43] Jesus said to him, *"Assuredly I tell you, today you will be with me in Paradise."*

The Death of Jesus
- **Matthew 27: 45-56 (Mark 15: 33-41; Luke 23: 44-49; John 19: 28-37)**

[45] Now from the sixth hour there was darkness over all the land until the ninth hour. [46] About the ninth hour Jesus cried with a loud voice, saying, *"Eli, Eli, lima sabachthani?"* That is, *"My God, my God, why have you forsaken me?"* [47] Some of them who stood there, when they heard it, said, "This man is calling Elijah." [48] Immediately one of them ran, and took a sponge, and filled it with vinegar, and put it on a reed, and gave him a drink. [49] The rest said, "Let him be. Let's see whether Elijah comes to save him." [50] Jesus cried again with a loud voice, and yielded up his spirit. [51] Behold, the veil of the temple was torn in two from the top to the bottom. The earth quaked and the rocks were split. [52] The tombs were opened, and many bodies of the saints who had fallen asleep were raised; [53] and coming out of the tombs after his resurrection, they entered into the holy city and appeared to many. [54] Now the centurion, and those who were with him watching Jesus, when they saw the earthquake, and the things that were done, feared exceedingly, saying, "Truly this was the Son of God." [55] Many women were there watching from afar, who had followed Jesus from Galilee, serving him. [56] Among them were Mary Magdalene, Mary the mother of James and Joses, and the mother of the sons of Zebedee.

The Burial of Jesus
- **Matthew 27: 57-61 (Mark 15: 42-47; Luke 23: 50-56; John 19: 38-42)**

[57] When evening had come, a rich man from Arimathaea, named Joseph, who himself was also Jesus' disciple came. [58] This man went to Pilate, and asked for Jesus' body. Then Pilate commanded the body to be given up. [59] Joseph took the body, and wrapped it in a clean linen cloth, [60] and laid it in his own new tomb, which he had cut out in the rock, and he rolled a great stone to the door of the tomb, and departed. [61] Mary Magdalene was there, and the other Mary, sitting opposite the tomb.

Guards at the Tomb
- **Matthew 27: 62-66**

[62] Now on the next day, which was the day after the Preparation Day, the chief priests and the Pharisees were gathered together to Pilate, [63] saying, "Sir, we remember what that deceiver said while he was still alive: 'After three days I will rise again.' [64] Command therefore that the tomb be made secure until the third day, lest perhaps his disciples come at night and steal him away, and tell the people, 'He is risen from the dead;' and the last deception will be worse than the first." [65] Pilate said to them, "You have a guard. Go, make it as secure as you can." [66] So they went with the guard and made the tomb secure, sealing the stone.

The Resurrection of Jesus
- **Matthew 28: 1-7 (Mark 16: 1-8; Luke 24: 1-12; John 20: 1-9)**

[1] Now after the Sabbath, as it began to dawn on the first day of the week, Mary Magdalene and the other Mary came to see the tomb. [2] Behold, there was a great earthquake, for an angel of the Lord descended from the sky, and came and rolled away the stone from the door, and sat on it. [3] His appearance was like lightning, and his clothing white as snow. [4] For fear of him, the guards shook, and became like dead men. [5] The angel answered the women, "Don't be afraid, for I know that you seek Jesus, who has been crucified. [6] He is not here, for he has risen, just like he said. Come, see the place where the Lord was lying. [7] Go quickly and tell his disciples, 'He has risen from the dead, and behold, he goes before you into Galilee; there you will see him.' Behold, I have told you."

Jesus Appears to Mary and Others
- **John 20: 10-18 (Matthew 28: 8-10; Mark 16: 9-11)**

[10] So the disciples went away again to their own homes. [11] But Mary was standing outside at the tomb weeping. So, as she wept, she stooped and looked into the tomb, [12] and she saw two angels in white sitting, one at the head, and one at the feet, where the body of Jesus had lain. [13] They told her, "Woman, why are you weeping?" She said to them, "Because they have taken away my Lord, and I don't know

where they have laid him." [14] When she had said this, she turned around and saw Jesus standing, and didn't know that it was Jesus. [15] Jesus said to her, *"Woman, why are you weeping? Who are you looking for?"* She, supposing him to be the gardener, said to him, "Sir, if you have carried him away, tell me where you have laid him, and I will take him away." [16] Jesus said to her, *"Mary."* She turned and said to him, "Rabboni!" which is to say, "Teacher!" [17] Jesus said to her, *"Don't hold me, for I haven't yet ascended to my Father; but go to my brothers, and tell them, 'I am ascending to my Father and your Father, to my God and your God.'"* [18] Mary Magdalene came and told the disciples that she had seen the Lord, and that he had said these things to her.

The Guard's Report
  • **Matthew 28: 11-15**

[11] Now while they were going, behold, some of the guards came into the city, and told the chief priests all the things that had happened. [12] When they were assembled with the elders, and had taken counsel, they gave a large amount of silver to the soldiers, [13] saying, "Say that his disciples came by night, and stole him away while we slept. [14] If this comes to the governor's ears, we will persuade him and make you free of worry." [15] So they took the money and did as they were told. This saying was spread abroad among the Jews, and continues until this day.

On the Road to Emmaus
  • **Luke 24: 13-35 (Mark 16: 12-13)**

[13] Behold, two of them were going that very day to a village named Emmaus, which was sixty stadia from Jerusalem. [14] They talked with each other about all of these things which had happened. [15] It happened, while they talked and questioned together, that Jesus himself came near, and went with them. [16] But their eyes were kept from recognizing him. [17] He said to them, *"What are you talking about as you walk, and are sad?"* [18] One of them, named Cleopas, answered him, "Are you the only stranger in Jerusalem who doesn't know the things which have happened there in these days?" [19] He said to them, *"What things?"* They said to him, "The things concerning Jesus,

the Nazarene, who was a prophet mighty in deed and word before God and all the people; [20] and how the chief priests and our rulers delivered him up to be condemned to death, and crucified him. [21] But we were hoping that it was he who would redeem Israel. Yes, and besides all this, it is now the third day since these things happened. [22] Also, certain women of our company amazed us, having arrived early at the tomb; [23] and when they didn't find his body, they came saying that they had also seen a vision of angels, who said that he was alive. [24] Some of us went to the tomb, and found it just like the women had said, but they didn't see him." [25] He said to them, *"Foolish men, and slow of heart to believe in all that the prophets have spoken! [26] Didn't the Christ have to suffer these things and to enter into his glory?"* [27] Beginning from Moses and from all the prophets, he explained to them in all the Scriptures the things concerning himself. [28] They drew near to the village, where they were going, and he acted like he would go further. [29] They urged him, saying, "Stay with us, for it is almost evening, and the day is almost over." He went in to stay with them. [30] It happened, that when he had sat down at the table with them, he took the bread and gave thanks. Breaking it, he gave to them. [31] Their eyes were opened, and they recognized him, and he vanished out of their sight. [32] They said one to another, "Weren't our hearts burning within us, while he spoke to us along the way, and while he opened the Scriptures to us?" [33] They rose up that very hour, returned to Jerusalem, and found the eleven gathered together, and those who were with them, [34] saying, "The Lord is risen indeed, and has appeared to Simon!" [35] They related the things that happened along the way, and how he was recognized by them in the breaking of the bread.

Jesus Appears to His Disciples
• **Luke 24: 36-43 (Mark 16: 14; John 20: 19-25)**
[36] As they said these things, Jesus himself stood among them, and said to them, *"Peace be to you."* [37] But they were terrified and filled with fear, and supposed that they had seen a spirit. [38] He said to them, *"Why are you troubled? Why do doubts arise in your hearts? [39] See my hands and my feet, that it is truly me. Touch me and see, for a spirit doesn't have flesh and bones, as you see that I have."*

[40] When he had said this, he showed them his hands and his feet. [41] While they still didn't believe for joy, and wondered, he said to them, *"Do you have anything here to eat?"* [42] They gave him a piece of a broiled fish and some honeycomb. [43] He took them, and ate in front of them.

Jesus Appears to Thomas
  • **John 20: 26-29**

[26] After eight days again his disciples were inside, and Thomas was with them. Jesus came, the doors being locked, and stood in the midst, and said, *"Peace be to you."* [27] Then he said to Thomas, *"Reach here your finger, and see my hands. Reach here your hand, and put it into my side. Don't be unbelieving, but believing."* [28] Thomas answered him, "My Lord and my God!" [29] Jesus said to him, *"Because you have seen me, you have believed. Blessed are those who have not seen, and have believed."*

The Purpose of John's Gospel
  • **John 20: 30-31**

[30] Therefore Jesus did many other signs in the presence of his disciples, which are not written in this book; [31] but these are written, that you may believe that Jesus is the Christ, the Son of God, and that believing you may have life in his name.

The Miraculous Catch of Fish
  • **John 21: 1-14**

[1] After these things, Jesus revealed himself again to the disciples at the sea of Tiberias. He revealed himself this way. [2] Simon Peter, Thomas called Didymus, Nathanael of Cana in Galilee, and the sons of Zebedee, and two others of his disciples were together. [3] Simon Peter said to them, "I'm going fishing." They told him, "We are also coming with you." They immediately went out, and entered into the boat. That night, they caught nothing. [4] But when day had already come, Jesus stood on the beach, yet the disciples didn't know that it was Jesus. [5] Jesus therefore said to them, *"Children, have you anything to eat?"* They answered him, "No." [6] He said to them, *"Cast the net on the right side of the boat, and you will find some."* They

cast it therefore, and now they weren't able to draw it in for the multitude of fish. [7] That disciple therefore whom Jesus loved said to Peter, "It's the Lord!" So when Simon Peter heard that it was the Lord, he wrapped his coat around him (for he was naked), and threw himself into the sea. [8] But the other disciples came in the little boat (for they were not far from the land, but about two hundred cubits away), dragging the net full of fish. [9] So when they got out on the land, they saw a fire of coals there, and fish laid on it, and bread. [10] Jesus said to them, *"Bring some of the fish which you have just caught."* [11] Simon Peter went up, and drew the net to land, full of great fish, one hundred fifty-three; and even though there were so many, the net wasn't torn. [12] Jesus said to them, *"Come and eat breakfast."* None of the disciples dared inquire of him, "Who are you?" knowing that it was the Lord. [13] Then Jesus came and took the bread, gave it to them, and the fish likewise. [14] This is now the third time that Jesus was revealed to his disciples, after he had risen from the dead.

Jesus Reinstates Peter
  • **John 21: 15-24**

[15] So when they had eaten their breakfast, Jesus said to Simon Peter, *"Simon, son of Jonah, do you love me more than these?"* He said to him, "Yes, Lord; you know that I have affection for you." He said to him, *"Feed my lambs."* [16] He said to him again a second time, *"Simon, son of Jonah, do you love me?"* He said to him, "Yes, Lord; you know that I have affection for you." He said to him, *"Tend my sheep."* [17] He said to him the third time, *"Simon, son of Jonah, do you have affection for me?"* Peter was grieved because he asked him the third time, *"Do you have affection for me?"* He said to him, "Lord, you know everything. You know that I have affection for you." Jesus said to him, *"Feed my sheep. [18] Most certainly I tell you, when you were young, you dressed yourself, and walked where you wanted to. But when you are old, you will stretch out your hands, and another will dress you, and carry you where you don't want to go."* [19] Now he said this, signifying by what kind of death he would glorify God. When he had said this, he said to him, *"Follow me."* [20] Then Peter, turning around, saw a disciple following. This was the

disciple whom Jesus sincerely loved, the one who had also leaned on Jesus' breast at the supper and asked, "Lord, who is going to betray You?" [21] Peter seeing him, said to Jesus, "Lord, what about this man?" [22] Jesus said to him, *"If I desire that he stay until I come, what is that to you? You follow me."* [23] This saying therefore went out among the brothers, that this disciple wouldn't die. Yet Jesus didn't say to him that he wouldn't die, but, *"If I desire that he stay until I come, what is that to you?"* [24] This is the disciple who testifies about these things, and wrote these things. We know that his witness is true.

The Great Commission
• Matthew 28: 16-20 (Mark 16: 15-18)
[16] But the eleven disciples went into Galilee, to the mountain where Jesus had sent them. [17] When they saw him, they bowed down to him, but some doubted. [18] Jesus came to them and spoke to them, saying, *"All authority has been given to me in heaven and on earth.* [19] *Go, and make disciples of all nations, baptizing them in the name of the Father and of the Son and of the Holy Spirit,* [20] *teaching them to observe all things that I commanded you. Behold, I am with you always, even to the end of the age."* Amen.

The Disciples Understand the Scriptures
• Luke 24: 44-49
[44] He said to them, *"This is what I told you, while I was still with you, that all things which are written in the law of Moses, the prophets, and the psalms, concerning me must be fulfilled."* [45] Then he opened their minds, that they might understand the Scriptures. [46] He said to them, *"Thus it is written, and thus it was necessary for the Christ to suffer and to rise from the dead the third day,* [47] *and that repentance and remission of sins should be preached in his name to all the nations, beginning at Jerusalem.* [48] *You are witnesses of these things.* [49] *Behold, I send forth the promise of my Father on you. But wait in the city of Jerusalem until you are clothed with power from on high."*

The Ascension of Jesus
- **Mark 16: 19-20 (Luke 24: 50-53)**

[19] So then the Lord, after he had spoken to them, was received up into heaven, and sat down at the right hand of God. [20] They went out, and preached everywhere, the Lord working with them, and confirming the word by the signs that followed. Amen.

The Mystery of Scripture
- **John 21: 25**

[25] There are also many other things which Jesus did, which if they would all be written, I suppose that even the world itself wouldn't have room for the books that would be written.

At A Glance

◎ ◎ ◎

Stories	M/P	Matthew	Mark	Luke	John
The Word Becomes Flesh					1: 1-5
The Birth of John the Baptist Foretold				1: 5-25	
The Birth of Jesus Foretold				1: 26-38	
Mary and Elizabeth				1: 39-56	
The Birth of John the Baptist				1: 57-80	
An Angel Appears Before Joseph		1: 18-25			
The Birth of Jesus				2: 1-7	
Shepherds and Angels				2: 8-20	

Stories	M/P	Matthew	Mark	Luke	John
Baby Jesus Presented at the Temple				2: 21-38	
Wise Men Visit the Messiah		2: 1-12			
Escape Into Egypt		2: 13-18			
Return to Nazareth		2: 19-23		2: 39-40	
The Boy Jesus at the Temple				2: 41-52	
Witness to the Light					1: 6-18
John the Baptist Prepares the Way		3: 1-12	1: 1-8	3: 1-17	1: 19-28
The Baptism of Jesus		3: 13-17	1: 9-11	3: 21-22	
John's Testimony					1: 29-34
Genealogy of Jesus (via Mary)				3: 23-38	
Genealogy of Jesus (via Joseph)		1: 1-17			
Temptation in the Wilderness		4: 1-11	1: 12-13	4: 1-13	
Jesus' First Disciples					1: 35-51

Stories	M/P	Matthew	Mark	Luke	John
Water Into Wine	M				2: 1-12
Jesus Clears the Temple Courts					2: 13-25
Jesus and Nicodemus					3: 1-21
John the Baptist Testifies About Jesus					3: 22-36
John the Baptist in Prison				3: 18-20	
A Samaritan Woman at the Well					4: 1-42
Jesus Begins Preaching		4: 12-17	1: 14-15	4: 14-15	4: 43-45
A Prophet Without Honor		13: 54-58	6: 1-6a	4: 16-30	
A Government Official's Son	M				4: 46-54
Jesus Drives out an Evil Spirit	M		1: 21-28	4: 31-37	
Jesus Heals Many People	M	8: 14-17	1: 29-34	4: 38-41	
Spreading the Good News		4: 23-25	1: 35-39	4: 42-44	
Fishers of Men	M	4: 18-22	1: 16-20	5: 1-11	

Stories	M/P	Matthew	Mark	Luke	John
Jesus Heals a Man with Leprosy	M	8: 1-4	1: 40-45	5: 12-16	
Jesus Heals a Paralyzed Man	M	9: 1-8	2: 1-12	5: 17-26	
Jesus Calls Matthew		9: 9-13	2: 13-17	5: 27-32	
Jesus Questioned About Fasting		9: 14-17	2: 18-22	5: 33-39	
At the Healing Pool	M				5: 1-15
Life Through the Son					5: 16-30
Testimonies About Jesus					5: 31-47
Lord of the Sabbath	M	12: 1-14	2: 23-28 & 3: 1-6	6: 1-11	
God's Chosen Servant		12: 15-21	3: 7-12		
The Beatitudes		5: 1-12		6: 17-26	
Salt and Light		5: 13-16			
Fulfillment of the Law		5: 17-20		16: 16-17	
Murder		5: 21-26			
Adultery		5: 27-30			

Stories	M/P	Matthew	Mark	Luke	John
Divorce		5: 31-32		16: 18	
Oaths		5: 33-37			
Love Your Enemies		5: 38-48		6: 27-30 & 32-36	
Giving to the Needy		6: 1-4			
Fasting		6: 16-18			
Treasures in Heaven		6: 19-24			
Do not Worry		6: 25-34		12: 22-34	
Judging Others		7: 1-6		6: 37-42	
The Golden Rule		7: 12		6: 31	
Narrow and Wide Gates		7: 13-14			
A Tree and its Fruit		7: 15-20		6: 43-45	
A Solid Foundation		7: 21-29		6: 46-49	
Faith of an Army Officer	M	8: 5-13		7: 1-10	
Jesus Raises a Widow's Son	M			7: 11-17	
Jesus and John the Baptist		11: 1-19		7: 18-35	

Stories	M/P	Matthew	Mark	Luke	John
Jesus Anointed by a Sinful Woman	P			7: 36-50	
Followers of Jesus				8: 1-3	
The Sower	P	13: 1-23	4: 1-20	8: 4-15	
The Weeds	P	13: 24-30 & 36-43			
Lamp on the Stand			4: 21-25	8: 16-18	
Jesus' Mother and Brothers		12: 46-50	3: 31-35	8: 19-21	
The Growing Seed	P		4: 26-29		
The Mustard Seed	P	13: 31-32	4: 30-32	13: 18-19	
The Yeast	P	13: 33		13: 20-21	
Speaking in Parables		13: 34-35	4: 33-34		
The Hidden Treasure	P	13: 44			
The Pearl	P	13: 45-46			
The Net	P	13: 47-51			
Knowledgeable Teachers		13: 52-53			

Stories	M/P	Matthew	Mark	Luke	John
Jesus Calms the Storm	M	8: 23-27	4: 35-41	8: 22-25	
Jesus Heals a Demon-Possessed Man	M	8: 28-34	5: 1-20	8: 26-39	
A Dead Girl	M	9: 18-19 & 23-26	5: 21-24 & 35-43	8: 40-42 & 49-56	
A Sick Woman	M	9: 20-22	5: 25-34	8: 43-48	
The Blind and Mute are Healed	M	9: 27-34			
The Workers are few		9: 35-38			
Jesus Appoints the Twelve Disciples		10: 1-4	3: 13-19	6: 12-16	
Jesus Sends out the Twelve Disciples		10: 5-42	6: 6b-13	9: 1-6	
John the Baptist Beheaded		14: 1-12	6: 14-29	9: 7-9	
Jesus Feeds the Five Thousand	M	14: 13-21	6: 30-44	9: 10-17	6: 1-15
Jesus Walks on Water	M	14: 22-33	6: 45-52		6: 16-21
All who Touched Him		14: 34-36	6: 53-56		

Stories	M/P	Matthew	Mark	Luke	John
The Bread of Life					6: 22-59
Many Disciples Desert Jesus					6: 60-71
Jesus' Brothers Disbelieve					7: 1-9
Jesus at the Feast of Tabernacles					7: 10-24
Division Over Jesus					7: 25-44
Unbelief of the Jewish Leaders					7: 45-53
An Adulterous Woman					8: 1-11
Light of the World					8: 12-20
Coming Judgment					8: 21-30
Children of Abraham					8: 31-41
Children of Satan					8: 42-47
Jesus' Claims About Himself					8: 48-59
Jesus Heals a Man Born Blind	M				9: 1-12

Stories	M/P	Matthew	Mark	Luke	John
The Pharisees Investigate the Healing					9: 13-34
Spiritual Blindness					9: 35-41
The Good Shepherd					10: 1-21
Conflict Over Jesus					10: 22-42
Clean and Unclean		15: 1-20	7: 1-23		
Faith of a Canaanite Woman	M	15: 21-28	7: 24-30		
Jesus Heals a Deaf and Mute Man	M	15: 29-31	7: 31-37		
Jesus Feeds the Four Thousand	M	15: 32-39	8: 1-10		
Demand for a Sign		16: 1-4	8: 11-13		
Beware of Some Teachings		16: 5-12	8: 14-21		
Jesus Heals a Blind Man	M		8: 22-26		
Peter Declares That Jesus is the Messiah		16: 13-20	8: 27-30	9: 18-20	

Stories	M/P	Matthew	Mark	Luke	John
Jesus Predicts His Own Death		16: 21-28	8: 31-38 & 9: 1	9: 21-27	
The Transfiguration		17: 1-13	9: 2-13	9: 28-36	
Jesus Heals a Boy With an Evil Spirit	M	17: 14-21	9: 14-29	9: 37-43a	
Jesus Predicts His Death a Second Time		17: 22-23	9: 30-32	9: 43b-45	
The Temple Tax	M	17: 24-27			
Greatest in the Kingdom of Heaven		18: 1-5	9: 33-37	9: 46-48	
Using the Name of Jesus			9: 38-41	9: 49-50	
Warnings Against Temptation		18: 6-11	9: 42-50	17: 1-2	
Dealing With Sin in the Church		18: 15-20			
The Unmerciful Servant	P	18: 21-35		17: 3-4	
Samaritan Opposition				9: 51-56	
The Cost of Following Jesus		8: 18-22		9: 57-62	

Stories	M/P	Matthew	Mark	Luke	John
Jesus Sends out Seventy Others		11: 20-30		10: 1-24	
The Good Samaritan	P			10: 25-37	
At the Home of Martha and Mary				10: 38-42	
How to Pray	P	6: 5-15		11: 1-8	
Ask, Seek & Knock		7: 7-11		11: 9-13	
Source of Power		12: 22-37	3: 20-30	11: 14-23	
A Miraculous Sign		12: 38-45		11: 24-32	
Lamp of the Body				11: 33-36	
The Religious Leaders are Criticized				11: 37-54	
Warnings and Encouragements				12: 1-12	
The Rich Fool	P			12: 13-21	
Watchfulness				12: 35-48	
Not Peace but Division				12: 49-53	
Interpreting the End Times				12: 54-59	

Stories	M/P	Matthew	Mark	Luke	John
Repent or Perish	P			13: 1-9	
A Woman is Healed on the Sabbath	M			13: 10-17	
The Narrow Door				13: 22-30	
At the Home of a Pharisee	M			14: 1-6	
Humility				14: 7-14	
The Great Banquet	P			14: 15-24	
The Cost of Becoming a Disciple				14: 25-35	
The Lost Sheep	P	18: 12-14		15: 1-7	
The Lost Coin	P			15: 8-10	
The Lost Son	P			15: 11-32	
The Wise Manager	P			16: 1-15	
The Rich Man and the Beggar	P			16: 19-31	
Sin, Faith & Duty	P			17: 5-10	
Jesus Heals Ten Lepers	M			17: 11-19	

Stories	M/P	Matthew	Mark	Luke	John
The Kingdom of God				17: 20-37	
The Persistent Widow	P			18: 1-8	
The Pharisee and the Tax Collector	P			18: 9-14	
Marriage and Divorce		19: 1-12	10: 1-12		
Jesus Blesses the Children		19: 13-15	10: 13-16	18: 15-17	
The Rich Young Ruler		19: 16-30	10: 17-31	18: 18-30	
The Vineyard Workers	P	20: 1-16			
Jesus Predicts His Death a Third Time		20: 17-19	10: 32-34	18: 31-34	
Serving Others		20: 20-28	10: 35-45		
A Blind Beggar Receives His Sight	M	20: 29-34	10: 46-52	18: 35-43	
The Tax Collector				19: 1-10	
The Ten Coins	P			19: 11-27	

Stories	M/P	Matthew	Mark	Luke	John
The Death and Resurrection of Lazarus	M				11: 1-44
A Plot to Kill Jesus		26: 1-5	14: 1-2	22: 1-2	11: 45-57
Jesus is Anointed at Bethany		26: 6-13	14: 3-9		12: 1-11
Judas Agrees to Betray Jesus		26: 14-16	14: 10-11	22: 3-6	
Jesus Enters Jerusalem		21: 1-11	11: 1-11	19: 28-44	12: 12-19
The Fruitless Fig Tree		21: 18-19a	11: 12-14		
Jesus Clears the Temple Again		21: 12-17	11: 15-19	19: 45-48	
The Withered Fig Tree	M	21: 19b-22	11: 20-26		
The Purpose of Jesus' Death					12: 20-36
Unbelief Among the Jews					12: 37-50
The Authority of Jesus is Questioned		21: 23-27	11: 27-33	20: 1-8	
The Two Sons	P	21: 28-32			
The Tenants	P	21: 33-46	12: 1-12	20: 9-19	

Stories	M/P	Matthew	Mark	Luke	John
The Wedding Feast	P	22: 1-14			
Paying Taxes to Caesar		22: 15-22	12: 13-17	20: 20-26	
The Resurrection and Marriage		22: 23-33	12: 18-27	20: 27-40	
The Greatest Commandments		22: 34-40	12: 28-34		
Whose Son is the Messiah?		22: 41-46	12: 35-37	20: 41-44	
Warnings Against Hypocrisy		23: 1-12	12: 38-40	20: 45-47	
Seven Woes		23: 13-36			
Jesus Grieves Over Jerusalem		23: 37-39		13: 31-35	
The Widow's Offering			12: 41-44	21: 1-4	
Jesus Teaches His Disciples		24: 1-35	13: 1-31	21: 5-33	
Signs of the End Times		24: 36-51	13: 32-37	21: 34-38	
The Ten Virgins	P	25: 1-13			
The Talents	P	25: 14-30			
The Sheep and the Goats		25: 31-46			

Stories	M/P	Matthew	Mark	Luke	John
Preparation for the Passover		26: 17-19	14: 12-16	22: 7-13	
The Last Supper					13: 1-17
The First Communion		26: 26-30	14: 22-26	22: 14-20	
Jesus Predicts His Betrayal		26: 20-25	14: 17-21	22: 21-23	13: 18-30
True Greatness				22: 24-30	
Jesus Predicts Peter's Denial		26: 31-35	14: 27-31	22: 31-34	13: 31-38
Jesus' Instructions to His Disciples				22: 35-38	
Jesus Comforts His Disciples					14: 1-4
The Way, the Truth, and the Life					14: 5-14
Promise of the Holy Spirit					14: 15-31
The Vine and its Branches					15: 1-17
The World Hates the Disciples					15: 18-27 & 16: 1-4
Work of the Holy Spirit					16: 5-16

Stories	M/P	Matthew	Mark	Luke	John
The Disciples Grief Will Change to Joy					16: 17-33
Jesus Prays for Himself					17: 1-5
Jesus Prays for His Disciples					17: 6-19
Jesus Prays for All Believers					17: 20-26
The Mount of Olives		26: 36-46	14: 32-42	22: 39-46	
Jesus is Arrested	M	26: 47-56	14: 43-52	22: 47-53	18: 1-14
Peter's First Denial of Jesus		26: 69-70	14: 66-68	22: 54-57	18: 15-17
Jesus Before the Council of Elders		26: 57-68	14: 53-65	22: 63-71	18: 18-24
Peter's Second & Third Denials		26: 71-75	14: 69-72	22: 58-62	18: 25-27
The Religious Leaders Condemn Jesus		27: 1-2	15: 1		
Judas Hangs Himself		27: 3-10			
Jesus Before Pilate and Herod		27: 11-26	15: 2-15	23: 1-25	18: 28-40

Stories	M/P	Matthew	Mark	Luke	John
The Soldiers Mock Jesus Again		27: 27-30	15: 16-20		19: 1-3
Jesus is Sentenced to Death					19: 4-16
The Crucifixion of Jesus		27: 31-44	15: 21-32	23: 26-43	19: 17-27
The Death of Jesus		27: 45-56	15: 33-41	23: 44-49	19: 28-37
The Burial of Jesus		27: 57-61	15: 42-47	23: 50-56	19: 38-42
Guards at the Tomb		27: 62-66			
The Resurrection of Jesus		28: 1-7	16: 1-8	24: 1-12	20: 1-9
Jesus Appears to Mary and Others		28: 8-10	16: 9-11		20: 10-18
The Guard's Report		28: 11-15			
On the Road to Emmaus			16: 12-13	24: 13-35	
Jesus Appears to His Disciples			16: 14	24: 36-43	20: 19-25
Jesus Appears to Thomas					20: 26-29

Stories	M/P	Matthew	Mark	Luke	John
The Purpose of John's Gospel					20: 30-31
The Miraculous Catch of Fish	M				21: 1-14
Jesus Reinstates Peter					21: 15-24
The Great Commission		28: 16-20	16: 15-18		
The Disciples Understand the Scriptures				24: 44-49	
The Ascension of Jesus			16: 19-20	24: 50-53	
The Mystery of Scripture					21: 25

Luke 1: 1-4 (Introduction)
M = Miracle / P = Parable
[   ] Suggested Reading Sequence

Becoming a Christian

◎ ◎ ◎

After reading *The Gospel Message* you should have a good understanding of Jesus Christ. Yet, scriptural knowledge alone is not sufficient for you to become a Christian - neither is attending church or simply believing that God exists. Salvation requires an act of faith. "Now faith is assurance of things hoped for, proof of things not seen" (Hebrews 11: 1).

God wants to establish a personal relationship with you through Jesus Christ. He moves our conscience in different ways, such as listening to a sermon or religious music, reading scripture, interacting with Christians, dreams, miracles, or by simply observing creation. *"No one can come to me [Jesus] unless the Father [God] who sent me draws him"* (John 6: 44a). Everyone gets an invitation, but few accept it. Will you? "The Lord is not slow in keeping his promise, as some understand slowness. Instead he is patient with you, not wanting anyone to perish, but everyone to come to repentance" (2 Peter 3: 9).

Sin is disobedience toward God. It includes our thoughts, attitudes, values, and behavior. Except for Jesus Christ, "All have sinned, and fall short of the glory of God" (Romans 3: 23). Sin results in death and without God's forgiveness, an eternity in Hell. "For the wages of sin is death, but the free gift of God is eternal life in Christ Jesus our Lord" (Romans 6: 23). People try to make peace with God by performing good works or living a moral life, but nothing can purify sin apart from the sacrificial blood of Jesus Christ. "For by grace you have been saved through faith, and that

175

not of yourselves; it is the gift of God, not of works, that no one would boast" (Ephesians 2: 8-9).

Jesus Christ died on a cross in payment for sin, and through His resurrection, paved the way for a future life in Heaven. *"For God so loved the world, that he gave his one and only Son, that whoever believes in him should not perish, but have eternal life"* (John 3: 16). The "world" means everyone, including you. "You [Jesus] are worthy to take the book, and to open its seals: for you were killed, and bought us for God with your blood, out of every tribe, language, people, and nation" (Revelation 5: 9). There is no other way for salvation to occur. Jesus said, *"I am the way, the truth, and the life. No one comes to the Father, except through me"* (John 14: 6). Although sinners do not deserve mercy, God gives it freely if we repent.

Are you ready to receive the gift of salvation? *"Behold, I stand at the door and knock. If anyone hears my voice and opens the door, then I will come in to him, and will dine with him, and he with me"* (Revelation 3: 20). After death, "The testimony is this, that God gave to us eternal life, and this life is in his Son. He who has the Son has the life. He who doesn't have God's Son doesn't have the life" (1 John 5: 11-12). So, if you are not a Christian when you die, you cannot change your mind later on. "Anyone whose name was not found written in the book of life was thrown into the lake of fire" (Revelation 20: 16).

"If you will confess with your mouth that Jesus is Lord, and believe in your heart that God raised him from the dead, you will be saved" (Romans 10: 9). This decision is the most important one that you will ever make in life. Once united with Christ, nothing can separate you from God's love (Romans 8: 38-39).

Glossary of Terms

⊙ ⊙ ⊙

Agnosticism is the belief that we cannot know for sure if there is a God or not.

Atheism is the belief that God does not exist.

Baptism refers to a sacrament or ordinance of the church intended to symbolize the death, burial, and resurrection of Jesus, and to identify an individual as part of a community of faith. Baptism is performed in various Christian communities by sprinkling, effusing (pouring), or immersing the individual with water.

Born Again: The Bible teaches that when we receive Jesus Christ as Lord and Savior, our lives are changed so much that we are called "new creatures."

Christ: His full name is the Lord Jesus Christ. The word "Christ" emphasizes that He is the anointed or specially chosen one of God to bring salvation to mankind by His death on the cross.

Communion (The Lord's Supper): Consists of eating a piece of unleavened bread (flat, with no yeast) and drinking either wine or unfermented grape juice, in the presence of other believers in remembrance of what Jesus has done for us when He died on the cross. The bread represents His body and the wine or juice represents His blood.

Conversion refers to the change that takes place when Christians receive Jesus Christ.

Conviction is used in two ways. When people have done things that are wrong, and the Holy Spirit reminds them that they have sinned, we say they are "under conviction." People who have never received Jesus Christ as their personal Lord and Savior sometimes fight conviction for a long time before they finally repent. Christians learn to repent quickly when the Holy Spirit brings conviction. Also, the word "conviction" is used to refer to strong beliefs upon which people base their lives.

Cult: Any group of people who claim to believe the Bible and Jesus Christ, but their teachings are not based on Christianity.

Demons are fallen angels who chose to be on Satan's side when he rebelled against God. God uses them, just as He uses Satan, to help Christians learn about spiritual warfare and preparation for eternal life.

Denomination: A Christian group that believes and practices things slightly different from other Christian groups. Individual churches are often part of a larger denomination. However, all Christian denominations agree that the Lord Jesus Christ is God who became man in order to die for our sin, and that faith in Him is the only way to receive eternal life.

Disciple: Someone who believes in and follows the teachings of Jesus Christ.

Doctrine: Teachings and principles that are taught in the Bible.

Evangelism means sharing the good news about Jesus Christ. The work of evangelism means telling people about what Jesus has done for them and providing them an opportunity to receive Jesus Christ as their personal Lord and Savior.

Faith is more than "head knowledge" about the truth of Jesus Christ. Faith means trusting Jesus Christ, and in Him alone, to save us from sin, death, and hell.

Fall of Man: God created Adam and Eve as sinless, innocent humans, but with the power to choose right from wrong. When Adam chose to disobey God, bringing sin into God's perfect creation, it led to an enormous change in the whole of creation, including the nature of mankind.

Glorification will take place one day for all Christians, but we will not experience it while we still live in these bodies of flesh and blood. When Jesus returns, Christians will be given new bodies that will be wonderful and eternal. These bodies are called "glorified" bodies, hence "glorification" will occur at that moment.

Gospel refers to the "good news" that Jesus Christ, God the Son, became a man like us. He lived a perfect and sinless life. He died on the cross to pay the penalty for our sin. He rose again and lives forever. He will forgive our sin and give us eternal life when we repent of our sin and put our faith in Him.

Grace is a gift from God that we do not deserve. The Bible teaches that all of us have sinned and deserve death and hell and that there is no way we can fix that problem on our own. But God gives us the gifts of forgiveness, righteousness, eternal life, peace, joy, the privilege of being part of His family, and many other wonderful things, even though we do not deserve them.

Heaven is a wonderful place that exists in the spirit world. We cannot see it or experience it with our senses. It is the place where God and His holy angels dwell. It is a place where continual worship of God occurs. When Christians die, their spirits go there to await the resurrection.

Hell: A place reserved for those who refuse God's offer of eternal life through Jesus Christ. The Bible teaches that it was prepared for

Satan and his angels, but it is for anyone who rejects Christ as well. The Bible describes hell as a place of unspeakable horror. The wonderful news is that God has provided a way for us to stay away from hell. When we accept Jesus Christ, He gives to us the gift of eternal life.

Holy Spirit: Is the third person in the Trinity (Father, Son, and Holy Spirit). The Holy Spirit comes to live inside us when we repent of our sin and receive Jesus Christ as our Lord and Savior. The Spirit gives us direction and wisdom for making life's decisions.

Hypocrisy means "pretense." People who claim to be living for Christ, but denying His power are guilty of hypocrisy. A person who condemns sins in others but excuses them in himself would be guilty of hypocrisy.

Invitation: God invites everyone to repent and to receive Jesus Christ as their personal Lord and Savior. Non-Christians are prompted to examine their own hearts and say "yes" to God's invitation.

Justification is the act of all our sins being forgiven and cleansed forever. This occurs the moment we receive Jesus Christ into our lives as Lord and Savior. When you are justified, it is like you have never sinned before. Since all our sins are forgiven and taken away, God declares us to be righteous.

Legalism has two meanings. It can refer to the belief of some people who are not Christians that salvation can occur through good works. It can also refer to Christians who cannot enjoy their freedom in Christ because they feel bound to do many things that God does not command us to do (or they feel bound *not* do things that God does not forbid us to do).

Lordship of Christ gives Jesus Christ total command of our lives. It makes no sense for anyone to claim that Jesus is their Savior and that He is God, but refuses to obey Him. When we receive Jesus Christ into our lives, we receive Him as Savior and as Lord.

Lost: Prior to receiving Jesus Christ as our personal Lord and Savior, we are said to be "lost." After we receive Jesus Christ we are "saved." Lost people do not have their sins forgiven until they repent and receive Christ. The Bible teaches that lost people are slaves to sin and to Satan. Lost people do not receive the gift of eternal life.

Mercy: Instead of giving us the punishment (death and hell) that we deserve, God has forgiven Christians and shown us mercy. Mercy and grace are two words that often go together. Grace is God giving us what we don't deserve and mercy is God *not* giving us what we *do* deserve.

Omnipotent means "all powerful." It is a word that describes God alone. He has perfect control over the entire universe. God has the power to do anything He chooses to do.

Omnipresent means that God is everywhere at the same time. Wherever we go, whatever we do, God is there with us all the time. At the same time, He is everywhere else with everyone else.

Omniscience means that God knows everything there is to know. There is nothing hidden from Him. God knows every detail about everyone on earth and everything about the entire universe.

Promptings of the Holy Spirit: When we receive the Lord Jesus Christ as our personal Lord and Savior, the Holy Spirit comes into our lives to give us wisdom and direction. He speaks by giving us thoughts to do the right thing. These thoughts are called "promptings of the Holy Spirit." His promptings will never contradict or disagree with God's Word, the Bible. The best way that new Christians can learn to recognize His voice is by studying the Bible. Of course, we often have our own thoughts. And some of these thoughts may be suggested to us by our enemy, Satan. As Christians mature, they learn to recognize the voice of the Holy Spirit apart from secular influences.

Reconciliation: Since God is completely holy and since men are sinners, there is a separation between mankind and God. Sin separates us from God. Jesus Christ paid the penalty for sin, making it possible for us to be forgiven. Being cleansed of sin makes it possible for us to be one with God again.

Redeemed: Slaves can be set free if someone with enough money pays the price for them. The free man essentially purchases the slave for himself and sets him free. Because of sin, we are slaves—slaves to sin and to Satan. When Jesus died on the cross, He paid the price for our sin. He purchased us from Satan. Therefore, we, who were once slaves, have been "redeemed."

Repent means to change one's mind and heart completely about sin. Before we become Christians, we may have a tendency to excuse our sins as if they were no big deal. But God says that when we come to Christ we must repent. We must see sin as God sees it—a destructive and deadly behavior that brings ruin into our lives and totally offends the loving God who made us.

Resurrection means to come back to life in such a way as to live forever and never die again. After His death and burial, the Lord Jesus Christ experienced resurrection. He came back to life and He lives forevermore. When Christians die, we also look forward to a resurrection. When the Lord Jesus Christ returns to earth, all Christians who have died will be resurrected to life in new glorified bodies to be with Him forever. The Bible teaches that, after the resurrection, we will have responsibilities, perfectly matched with the skills and gifts God has given us, to serve the Lord Jesus Christ in His exciting kingdom on earth.

Salvation refers to the fact that God has rescued, or saved, us from sin and from its consequences (death). In the Bible, we see three aspects of salvation—justification, sanctification, and glorification.

Salvation (Assurance of): When we receive Jesus Christ as savior, He promises that nothing can ever separate us from His love or take us out of His hand. We can be confident that when we die, we will be with Him forever.

Sanctification is that process by which God sets those who have received Jesus Christ apart from the world and from sin to accomplish His purpose. When we experience Christian growth and become more like Jesus, we are experiencing sanctification. Similar to holiness.

Satan was one of the greatest angels ever created by God. He was so great and so wonderful that he became full of pride and rebelled against God. God could have destroyed Satan immediately, but God chose to use Satan as a way for Christians to battle, and overcome temptation. Satan knows the only way he can hurt God is through tempting Christians them to sin against God. Christians know that Satan was ultimately defeated when Jesus died on the cross.

Saved: The most common word used to describe Christians. When we receive Jesus Christ, He saves us from slavery to sin, death, and hell. Although our physical bodies will decay, our spirit will not. Christians have no reason to fear death or hell since Jesus saved us from these things.

Sin is disobedience toward God, often referred to as missing the mark. God has told us in His Word how we should live, but all of us have chosen to disobey Him. When we act selfishly; when we rebel against God; when we tell lies; lose our temper; lust; get irritated at others; etc—we have sinned. Sin always leads to hurt and pain for ourselves and others. Eventually sin leads to death and destruction. We cannot "fix" our sin problem by trying to be good. That's why Jesus Christ died on the cross—to pay the death penalty for our sins. When we repent of our sin and place our faith in God, He forgives and cleanses us.

Spiritual Warfare: All Christians have a common enemy—Satan and his demons. God commands us, as part of our preparation for eternity, to resist and overcome the evil one. In His word, God has given us weapons which He commands us to use for that purpose.

Temptation is the suggestion that it would be good to do something that God says is sin. Some people feel guilty because they are tempted to do sinful things. But temptation is nothing to feel guilty about. Even Jesus was tempted. Temptation simply means that we have a battle to fight. We can choose to do the right thing and win the battle over temptation. Or we can choose to sin. One of the best ways to win against temptation is to memorize Bible verses.

Trinity: The Bible teaches that God reveals Himself as one God who exists as three persons: God the Father, God the Son, and God the Holy Spirit. The word "Trinity" combines the prefix "tri" (meaning three) with the word "unity" (meaning one).

Washed in the Blood: The word "washed" means to become clean. The blood refers to the fact that Jesus died on the cross, giving up His blood for us. When we receive Jesus Christ, he forgives us of our sins and declares us to be righteous on the basis of His precious blood that was shed for us. To be washed in His blood means that our sins have been forgiven because we have trusted in the sacrifice of Himself on the cross.

Worship means to give our highest devotion, love, service, and praise to something or someone. To worship means that we rank that person or thing as most important in our life. Christians believe that it is important to worship God alone. The Bible says that when we allow any other person or thing to become more important to us than God, we have committed the sin of idolatry. Christians meet together frequently in order to worship God. These meetings are not just for fellowship and learning. They are primarily so that we can personally express with others our praise and adoration of God through words and music.

Some terms slightly modified, all used with permission. Abounding Joy. http://www.aboundingjoy.com/index.html

CPSIA information can be obtained at www.ICGtesting.com
Printed in the USA
LVOW062315050312

271473LV00005B/2/P